BEST

PLAYS

Introductory Level

7 Plays for Young People

with Lessons for Teaching the Basic Elements of Literature

JAMESTOWN  PUBLISHERS

a division of NTC/CONTEMPORARY PUBLISHING GROUP
Lincolnwood, Illinois USA

Cover Design: Steve Strauss   **Cover Illustration:** Michael Steirnagle
Interior Design: Steve Strauss   **Interior Illustration:** Jude Macaren

ISBN: 0-89061-902-6 (hardbound)
ISBN: 0-89061-875-5 (softbound)

Published by Jamestown Publishers,
a division of NTC/Contemporary Publishing Group, Inc.
4255 West Touhy Avenue, Lincolnwood (Chicago), Illinois 60646-1975, U.S.A.

8 9 0 QB 0 9 8 7 6 5 4 3 2 1

ACKNOWLEDGMENTS

Acknowledgment is gratefully made to the following publishers, authors, and agents for permission to reprint these works. Every effort has been made to determine copyright owners. In the case of any omissions, the Publisher will be pleased to make suitable acknowledgments in future editions.

Excerpts from *A Young Lady of Property* by Horton Foote. Copyright © 1955 by Horton Foote. Copyright © Renewed 1981 by Horton Foote. CAUTION: The reprinting of *A Young Lady of Property* included in this volume is reprinted by permission of the author and The Barbara Hogenson Agency. The amateur and stock performance rights in this play are controlled exclusively by Dramatists Play Service, Inc., 440 Park Avenue South, New York, NY 10016. No amateur or stock production of the play may be given without obtaining in advance the written permission of the Dramatists Play Service, Inc., and paying the requisite fee. Inquiries regarding all other rights should be addressed to Barbara Hogenson, The Barbara Hogenson Agency, 165 West End Avenue, Suite 19-C, New York, NY 10023.

Back There by Rod Serling. Reprinted by permission of The Rod Serling Trust. All rights reserved. © 1960 Rod Serling; © 1988 by Carolyn Serling, Jodi Serling, and Anne Serling.

When the Rattlesnake Sounds by Alice Childress. Copyright © 1975 by Alice Childress. Used by permission of Flora Roberts, Inc.

Excerpt from *I Remember Mama: A Play in Two Acts* by John Van Druten. Copyright 1945 by John Van Druten and renewed 1972 by Carter Lodge, reprinted by permission of Harcourt Brace & Company.

The Monkey's Paw by W. W. Jacobs. Dramatized by Harriet Dexter. Reprinted by permission from *Plays, the Drama Magazine for Young People*. Copyright © 1983 by Plays, Inc., Publishers, Boston, MA.

Let Me Hear You Whisper by Paul Zindel. Text copyright © 1970 by Paul Zindel. Used by permission of HarperCollins Publishers.

Rip Van Winkle by Washington Irving. Adapted by Adele Thane. Reprinted by permission from *Plays, the Drama Magazine for Young People*. Copyright © 1966, 1977, 1983 by Plays, Inc., Publishers, Boston, MA.

CONTENTS

TO THE STUDENT

A play, or drama, is a kind of literature in which actors take the roles of characters, speak their words, and act out their movements to tell a story. Probably the first dramas were presented by ancient hunters who came back to their caves and impressed their families by acting out the adventure of the hunt.

As cultures developed, so did drama. Peoples in every part of the world created their own styles of presenting stories through speaking and acting. Poetry and songs, stylized movements and dance, stunning costumes, and elaborate scenery have all been made a part of plays. Over time, we have adapted play techniques to changing technology. Now, what was once acted out for a small group in front of a campfire can be filmed and shown in theaters or on television around the world. But at the heart of drama is still what the cave dwellers enjoyed: seeing an interesting, exciting story acted out.

You are about to read plays by some of the best playwrights in the world. You will read the descriptions of the sets, the words assigned to the actors, and the directions for their movements. With your imagination, you can bring the characters and scenes to life.

Reading the plays, rather than seeing them, has certain disadvantages. You don't get to look at the scenery, hear the sound effects, respond to the actors, and experience all the other things that go into live theater. Reading the plays does have its advantages, however. You can observe more carefully how the characters interact. You can learn from the stage directions what the playwright considers essential. You can reread favorite parts and imagine how you would cast actors and stage the scenes. You become the director and producer of each play you read, working with the playwright to bring his or her words to life.

As you read the plays in this book, you will be able to see how the writers constructed them. You will learn about the elements of a play and study the techniques that play-wrights use to create imaginary worlds for their audiences. You also will have a chance to try these techniques in your own writing.

UNIT FORMAT AND ACTIVITIES

- Each unit begins with an illustration of a scene from the play you will read. This illustration will help you understand or make some predictions about the play.
- The introduction begins with information about the play and its author. If the play is based on another piece of writing, there is also information about the author of the original work. The introduction then presents an important literary concept and gives you an opportunity to develop this concept in your own writing. Finally, there are questions for you to consider as you read.
- The text of the play makes up the next section. In a few cases, the selection consists of only one act or a sequence of scenes from a longer play.
- Following each play are questions that test your comprehension of events and other elements of the play as well as your critical thinking skills. Your answers to these questions and to other exercises in the unit should be recorded in a personal literature notebook. Check your answers with your teacher.
- Your teacher may provide you with charts to record your progress in developing your comprehension skills: The Comprehension Skills Graph *records* your scores and the Comprehension Skills Profile *analyzes* your scores—providing you with information about the skills on which you need to focus. Your teacher will discuss ways to work on those comprehension skills.

- The next section contains three lessons and begins with a discussion of the literary concept that is the unit's focus. Each lesson illustrates a technique that the author uses to develop the concept. For example, you will see how a playwright uses stage directions, dialogue, and action to create characters.
- Short-answer exercises test your understanding of the author's techniques, as illustrated by short excerpts from the play. You can check your answers to the exercises with your teacher and determine what you need to review.
- Each lesson also includes a writing exercise that guides you in creating your own original work using the techniques you have just studied.
- Discussion guides and a final writing activity round out each unit in the book. These activities will help sharpen your reading, thinking, speaking, and writing skills.

Reading the plays in this book will enable you to recognize and appreciate the skills it takes to write an entertaining play. When you understand what makes a play good, you will become a better reader and a better viewer. The writing exercises and assignments will help you become a better writer by giving you practice in using the authors' techniques to make your own plays interesting.

UNIT 1

How to Read a Play

A Young Lady of Property

by Horton Foote

INTRODUCTION

The selection you are about to read is from the middle of a play called *A Young Lady of Property*. The play is set in 1925. Fifteen-year-old Wilma Thompson feels that her life lacks excitement and adventure. She and her best friend Arabella have written to a Hollywood director who is offering screen tests to "people of beauty and talent" who want to be in the movies. The girls are anxiously waiting to hear from the director so they can leave their hometown of Harrison, Texas, and head for Hollywood.

Wilma lives with her Aunt Gert, who is her father's sister. Before Wilma's mother died, she made Wilma's father promise that the family home would go to Wilma. Wilma associates her "property" with the good times she had there with her mother when Wilma was very young. She is proud that she owns a house, even though her father, Lester, rents it out and pockets the rent money himself.

For a long time, Wilma was angry with her father because of his gambling problem, but now she believes he has reformed, and she admits that she loves him. She would be happy to give up her dream of going to Hollywood if she could live with him again in her house. However, her father has been keeping company with a local woman, Mrs. Leighton, and the town gossips are sure that the two are planning to marry soon. Although Wilma knows Mrs. Leighton only by sight, she is sure that she could never love her and suspects that Mrs. Leighton is trapping her father into marriage. Wilma believes that her father's remarriage could ruin her dream of living in the family home with him again.

Just before this selection begins, Aunt Gert finds out that her brother is definitely going to marry Mrs. Leighton. Everyone, including the housekeeper, Minna, is worried about how Wilma will take the news. At the same time, Arabella receives the long-awaited letters from the Hollywood director and brings them to Aunt Gert's house so the two girls can open them together, but Wilma is not there. Instead she has gone to the house she owns because she "feels the need of seeing it." As the excerpt you are about to read begins, Arabella enters Wilma's yard with the letters in her hand.

ABOUT THE AUTHOR

Horton Foote was born in 1916 in Wharton, Texas. As a young man, he studied acting and performed in summer theater for a few years. However, his first love was—and still is—play writing. He has written a number of fine plays for the stage, television, and films. Many of his original plays take place in the fictional town of Harrison, Texas, a setting that bears an unmistakable likeness to the town where he grew up.

Horton Foote won Academy Awards for his screenplay *Tender Mercies* and his movie adaptation of the novel *To Kill a Mockingbird,* for which he also won the Writer's Guild of America award in 1962. In 1995, he was awarded the Pulitzer Prize for drama for *The Young Man from Atlanta.*

Foote's play *A Young Lady of Property* was first presented as a television play, or teleplay, on Philco Television Playhouse in 1953.

ABOUT THE LESSONS

The lessons that follow this excerpt from *A Young Lady of Property* focus on how to read a play. Plays are written to be performed in front of an audience. If you waited for every play to be performed by a group of actors, however, you would miss out on some excellent writing. As a reader, you can enjoy every play ever written by reading it yourself. However, reading a play takes special skills. The playwright has included everything you need in order to understand the play, but it takes an active, involved reader to get the most out of it. The lessons will introduce you to the best ways to read a play.

 WRITING: PREPARING TO WRITE A SCENE

At the end of this unit, you will write a short scene for a play. You will use the format that playwrights traditionally use for stage plays. The suggestions below will help you get started:

- Try to remember plays that you have seen, either performed by your classmates or by professional actors. Make a list of these plays.
- Now choose the play that you remember best. Try to picture just one scene—the people and things you could see at a single moment. Who was on stage? What were they doing? Make some notes about what you saw.
- Using your notes as a guide, draw a diagram of the stage as you remember it. If you don't feel comfortable drawing the actors and the scenery, just write in the names of the things you saw. See the example on the following page:

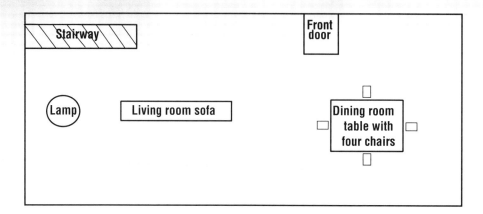

AS YOU READ

Think about these questions as you read the selection. They will give you ideas for what to think about and look for as you learn to read a play.

- How does the format of a play differ from the format of a short story or novel? Why is it different?
- How does the playwright help you picture the stage, the movements of the actors, and the action of the play?
- How does the playwright help you "hear" the words of the characters as they are meant to be spoken?

A Young Lady of Property

by Horton Foote

STAGE

The stage is divided into four areas. Area one, directly across the front of the stage, is a sidewalk. Area two, just above the sidewalk L. of C., is part of a kitchen. A table, with a portable phonograph on it, and four chairs are placed here. Area three is above the sidewalk R. of C. It has a yard swing in it. Area four is directly U.C. In it is a post office window.

(. . . The lights fade in the area D.L. *as they come up on the area* D.R. **Wilma** *comes in from* U.C. *of the* D.R. *area. It is the yard of her house. She sits in the swing rocking back and forth, singing "Birmingham Jail" in her hillbilly style.* **Arabella** *comes running in* R.C. *of the yard area.)*

Wilma.   Heh, Arabella. Come sit and swing.

Arabella.   All right. Your letter came.

Wilma.   Whoopee. Where is it?

Arabella.   Here. *(She gives it to her.* **Wilma** *tears it open. She reads:)*

Wilma.   "Dear Miss Thompson: Mr. Delafonte will be glad to see you anytime next week about your contemplated[1] screen test. We suggest you call the office when you arrive in the city and we will set an exact time. Yours truly, Adele Murray." Well . . . Did you get yours?

Arabella.   Yes.

Wilma.   What did it say?

Arabella.   The same.

Wilma.   Exactly the same?

Arabella.   Yes.

---

[1] planned or considered

Wilma. Well, let's pack our bags. Hollywood, here we come.

Arabella. Wilma . . .

Wilma. Yes?

Arabella. I have to tell you something. . . . Well . . . I . . .

Wilma. What is it?

Arabella. Well . . . promise me you won't hate me, or stop being my friend. I never had a friend, Wilma, until you began being nice to me, and I couldn't stand it if you weren't my friend any longer. . . .

Wilma. Oh, my cow. Stop talking like that. I'll never stop being your friend. What do you want to tell me?

Arabella. Well . . . I don't want to go to see Mr. Delafonte, Wilma. . . .

Wilma. You don't?

Arabella. No. I don't want to be a movie star. I don't want to leave Harrison or my mother or father. . . . I just want to stay here the rest of my life and get married and settle down and have children.

Wilma. Arabella. . .

Arabella. I just pretended like I wanted to go to Hollywood because I knew you wanted me to, and I wanted you to like me. . . .

Wilma. Oh, Arabella . . .

Arabella. Don't hate me, Wilma. You see, I'd be afraid . . . I'd die if I had to go to see Mr. Delafonte. Why, I even get faint when I have to recite before the class. I'm not like you. You're not scared of anything.

Wilma. Why do you say that?

Arabella. Because you're not. I know.

Wilma. Oh, yes, I am. I'm scared of lots of things.

Arabella. What?

Wilma.   Getting lost in a city. Being bitten by dogs. Old lady Leighton taking my daddy away. . . . *(a pause)*

Arabella.   Will you still be my friend?

Wilma.   Sure. I'll always be your friend.

Arabella.   I'm glad. Oh, I almost forgot. Your Aunt Gert said for you to come on home.

Wilma.   I'll go in a little. I love to swing in my front yard. Aunt Gert has a swing in her front yard, but it's not the same. Mama and I used to come out here and swing together. Some nights when Daddy was out all night gambling, I used to wake up and hear her out here swinging away. Sometimes she'd let me come and sit beside her. We'd swing until three or four in the morning. *(A pause. She looks out into the yard.)* The pear tree looks sickly, doesn't it? The fig trees are doing nicely though. I was out in back and the weeds are near knee high, but fig trees just seem to thrive in the weeds. The freeze must have killed off the banana trees. . . . *(A pause. **Wilma** stops swinging—she walks around the yard.)* Maybe I won't leave either. Maybe I won't go to Hollywood after all.

Arabella.   You won't?

Wilma.   No. Maybe I shouldn't. That just comes to me now. You know sometimes my old house looks so lonesome it tears at my heart. I used to think it looked lonesome just whenever it had no tenants, but now it comes to me it has looked lonesome ever since Mama died and we moved away, and it will look lonesome until some of us move back here. Of course, Mama can't, and Daddy won't. So it's up to me.

Arabella.   Are you gonna live here all by yourself?

Wilma.   No. I talk big about living here by myself, but I'm too much of a coward to do that. But maybe I'll finish school and live with Aunt Gert and keep on renting the house until I meet some nice boy with good habits and steady ways, and marry him. Then we'll move here and have children and I bet this old house won't be lonely anymore. I'll get Mama's old croquet set and put it out under the pecan trees and play croquet with my children, or sit in this yard and swing and wave to people as they pass by.

Arabella. Oh, I wish you would. Mama says that's a normal life for a girl, marrying and having children. She says being an actress is all right, but the other's better.

Wilma. Maybe I've come to agree with your mama. Maybe I was going to Hollywood out of pure lonesomeness. I felt so alone with Mrs. Leighton getting my daddy and my mama having left the world. Daddy could have taken away my lonesomeness, but he didn't want to or couldn't. Aunt Gert says nobody is lonesome with a house full of children, so maybe that's what I just ought to stay here and have. . . .

Arabella. Have you decided on a husband yet?

Wilma. No.

Arabella. Mama says that's the bad feature of being a girl, you have to wait for the boy to ask you and just pray that the one you want wants you. Tommy Murray is nice, isn't he?

Wilma. I think so.

Arabella. Jay Godfrey told me once he wanted to ask you for a date, but he didn't dare because he was afraid you'd turn him down.

Wilma. Why did he think that?

Arabella. He said the way you talked he didn't think you would go out with anything less than a movie star.

Wilma. Maybe you'd tell him different. . . .

Arabella. All right. I think Jay Godfrey is very nice. Don't you?

Wilma. Yes, I think he's very nice and Tommy is nice. . . .

Arabella. Maybe we could double-date sometimes.

Wilma. That might be fun.

Arabella. Oh, Wilma. Don't go to Hollywood. Stay here in Harrison and let's be friends forever. . . .

Wilma. All right. I will.

Arabella. You will?

Wilma. Sure, why not? I'll stay here. I'll stay and marry and live in my house.

Arabella. Oh, Wilma. I'm so glad. I'm so very glad. (**Wilma** *gets back in the swing. They swing vigorously[2] back and forth. . . . A* **Man** *comes in R.C. of the yard area.*)

Man. I beg your pardon. Is this the Thompson house? (*They stop swinging.*)

Wilma. Yes sir.

Man. I understand it's for sale. I'd like to look around.

Wilma. No sir. It's not for sale. It's for rent. I'm Wilma Thompson. I own the house. My daddy rents it for me. . . .

Man. Oh, well, we were told by Mr. Mavis . . .

Wilma. I'm sure. Mr. Mavis tries to sell everything around here. He's pulled that once before about our house, but this house is not for sale. It's for rent.

Man. You're sure?

Wilma. I'm positive. We rent it for twenty-seven fifty a month. You pay lights, water and keep the yard clean. We are very particular over how the yard is kept. I'd be glad to show it to you. . . .

Man. I'm sorry. I was interested in buying. There must have been a mistake.

Wilma. There must have been.

---

[2] in a lively or energetic way

Man.   Where could I find your father, young lady?

Wilma.   Why do you want to see him?

Man.   Well, I'd just like to get this straight. I understood from Mr. Mavis . . .

Wilma.   Mr. Mavis has nothing to do with my house. My house is for rent, not for sale.

Man.   All right. (*The* **Man** *leaves. He goes out* R.C. *of the yard area.*)

Wilma.   The nerve of old man Mavis putting out around town that my house is for sale. Isn't that nervy, Arabella? (**Arabella** *gets out of the swing.*)

Arabella.   We'd better go. It'll be dark soon. The tree frogs are starting.

Wilma.   It just makes me furious. Wouldn't it make you furious?

Arabella.   Come on. Let's go.

Wilma.   Wouldn't it make you furious?

Arabella.   Yes.

Wilma.   You don't sound like you mean it.

Arabella.   Well . . .

Wilma.   Well . . . what? . . .

Arabella.   Nothing. . . . Let's go.

Wilma.   Arabella, you know something you're not telling me.

Arabella.   No, I don't. Honest, Wilma. . . .

Wilma.   You do. Look at me, Arabella . . .

Arabella.   I don't know anything. I swear . . .

Wilma.   You do. I thought you were my friend.

Arabella.   I am. I am.

Wilma.   Well, then why don't you tell me?

Arabella.   Because I promised not to.

Wilma. Why?

Arabella. Well . . . I . . .

Wilma. What is it? Arabella, please tell me.

Arabella. Well . . . Will you never say I told you?

Wilma. I swear.

Arabella. Well, I didn't tell you before because in all the excitement in telling you I wasn't going to Hollywood and your saying you weren't going, I forgot about it . . . until that man came . . .

Wilma. What is it, Arabella? What is it?

Arabella. Well, I heard my daddy tell my mother that Mr. Lester had taken out a license to marry Mrs. Leighton.

Wilma. Oh, well. That doesn't surprise me too much. I've been looking for that to happen.

Arabella. But that isn't all, Wilma. . . .

Wilma. What else?

Arabella. Well . . .

Wilma. What else?

Arabella. Well . . .

Wilma. What else, Arabella? What else? . . .

Arabella. Well . . . My daddy heard that your daddy had put this house up for sale. . . .

Wilma. I don't believe you. . . .

Arabella. That's what he said, Wilma. . . . I . . . He said Mr. Lester came to him and wanted to know if he wanted to buy it. . . .

Wilma. Well. He won't do it. Not my house. He won't do it! (**Wilma** *has jumped out of the swing and runs out of the yard* U.C.)

Arabella. Wilma . . . Wilma . . . Please . . . don't say I said it. . . . Wilma . . . (*She is standing alone and frightened as the lights fade. The lights are brought up in the* *area* L. *of* C. **Minna** *is mixing some dough on the table.* **Miss Gert** *comes in.*)

Gert.   She's not back yet?

Minna.   No. I knew when Arabella took that letter over there she wouldn't be here until good dark.

Gert.   I just put in a call for Lester. . . . He is going to have to tell her about the marriage. It's his place. Don't you think so?

Minna.   I certainly do. I most certainly do. (**Wilma** *comes running in* U.C. *of the kitchen area.*)

Wilma.   Aunt Gert, do you know where I can find my daddy?

Gert.   No, Wilma . . . I . . .

Wilma.   Well, I've got to find him. I went over to the cotton gin but he'd left. I called out to his boardinghouse and he wasn't there. . . .

Gert.   Well, I don't know, Wilma. . . .

Wilma.   Is he gonna sell my house?

Gert.   Wilma . . .

Wilma.   Is he or isn't he?

Gert.   I don't know anything about it. . . .

Wilma.   Well, something's going on. Let me tell you that. I was sitting in the swing with Arabella when a man came up and said he wanted to buy it, and I said to rent and he said to buy, that Mr. Mavis had sent him over, and I told him he was mistaken and he left. Well, I was plenty mad at Mr. Mavis and told Arabella so, but she looked funny and I got suspicious and I finally got it out of her that Daddy was going to marry old lady Leighton and was putting my house up for sale. . . . (**Gert** *is crying.*) Aunt Gert. Isn't that my house?

Gert.   Yes. I'd always thought so. . . .

Wilma.   Then he can't do it. Don't let him do it. It's my house. It's all in this world that belongs to me. Let Mrs. Leighton take him if she wants to, but not my house. Please, please, please. (*She is crying.* **Minna** *goes to her.*)

Minna. Now, come on, honey. Come on, baby. . . .

Wilma. I wouldn't sell it, not even to get me to Hollywood. I thought this afternoon, before the letter from Mr. Delafonte came, I'd ask Aunt Gert to let me sell it, and go on off, but when I went over there and sat in my yard and rocked in my swing and thought of my mama and how lonesome the house looked since we moved away . . . I knew I couldn't . . . I knew I never would. . . . I'd never go to Hollywood before I'd sell that house, and he can't. . . . I won't let him. I won't let him.

Minna. Now, honey . . . honey . . . Miss Gert, do you know anything about this?

Gert. (*wiping her eyes*) Minna, I don't. I heard at the card party that he was marrying Mrs. Leighton . . . but I heard nothing about Lester's selling the house. . . .

Minna. Well, can he? . . .

Gert. I don't know. I just never thought my brother, my own brother . . . Oh, I just can't stand things like this. You see, it's all so mixed up. I don't think there was anything said in writing about Wilma's having the house, but it was clearly Alice's intention. She called me in the room before Lester and made him promise just before she died that he would always have the house for Wilma. . . .

Minna. Well, why don't we find out? . . .

Gert. Well . . . I don't know how. . . . I left a message for Lester. I can't reach him.

Minna. I'd call Mr. Bill if I were you. He's a lawyer.

Gert. But, Minna, my brother.

Minna. I'd call me a lawyer, brother or no brother. If you don't, I will. I'm not gonna have what belongs to this child stolen from her by Mr. Lester or anybody else. . . .

Gert.   All right. I will. I'll go talk to Bill. I'll find out what we can do legally. (*She starts out* D.L. *of the area.* **Lester** *comes in* U.C. *of the area.* **Minna** *sees him coming.*)

Minna.   Miss Gert. (**Gert** *turns and sees him just as he gets inside the area.*)

Lester.   Hello, Gert.

Gert.   Hello, Lester.

Lester.   Hello, Wilma.

Wilma.   Hello . . .

Gert.   Wilma, I think you'd better leave. . . .

Wilma.   Yes'm. . . . (*She starts out.*)

Lester.   Wait a minute, Gert. I've something to tell you all. I want Wilma to hear. . . .

Gert.   I think we know already. Go on, Wilma.

Wilma.   Yes'm. (**Wilma** *leaves* D.L. *of the area.* **Minna** *follows after her. A pause.*)

Gert.   We've heard about the marriage, Lester.

Lester.   Oh, well. I'm sorry I couldn't be the one to tell you. We only decided this morning. There was a lot to do, a license and some business to attend to. I haven't told anyone. I don't know how the news got out.

Gert.   You didn't really expect them to keep quiet about it at the courthouse?

Lester.   Oh. Well, of course I didn't think about that. (*a pause*) Well, the other thing is . . . You see . . . I've decided to sell the house.

Gert.   I know. Wilma just found out about that, too.

Lester.   Oh. Well, I'll explain the whole thing to you. You see, I felt . . . (**Gert** *starts to cry.*) Now what's the matter with you, Gert?

Gert.   To think that my brother, my own brother, would do something like this.

Lester.   Like what? After all it's my house, Gert.

Gert.   There's some dispute about that. The least I think you could have done, the very least, was come to tell your own child.

Lester.   Well, I'm here now to do that. I only put it up for sale at noon today. I've nothing to hide or be ashamed of. The house is in my name. Sibyl, Mrs. Leighton, doesn't like Harrison. You can't blame her. People have been rotten to her. We're moving to Houston. I'm selling this house to pay down on one in Houston. That'll belong to Wilma just the same, someday. Sibyl's agreed to that, and Wilma will really get a better house in time. And we always want her to feel like it's her home, come and visit us summers . . . and like I say when something happens to me or Sibyl the house will be hers. . . .

Gert.   That's not the point, Lester. . . .

Lester.   What do you mean?

Gert.   You know very well.

Lester.   I can't make a home for her over there, can I? She'll be grown soon and marrying and having her own house. I held on to this place as long as I could. . . . Well, I'm not going to feel guilty about it. . . .

Gert.   I'm going to try to stop you, Lester. . . .

Lester.   Now look, Gert. For once try and be sensible. . . .

Gert.   Legally I'm going to try and stop you. I'm going . . .

Lester.   Please, Gert . . .

Gert.   . . . to call Bill and tell him the whole situation and see what we can do. If we have any rights I'll take it to every court I can. Brother or no brother. . . .

Lester.   Now look, don't carry on like this. Maybe I've handled it clumsily and if I have I'm sorry. I just didn't think. . . . I should have, I know . . . but I . . .

Gert.   That's right. You didn't think. You never do. Well, this time you're going to have to. . . .

Lester.   Can't you look at it this way? Wilma is getting a better house and . . .

Gert.   Maybe she doesn't want a better house. Maybe she just wants this one. But that isn't the point either. The sickening part is that you really didn't care what Wilma thought, or even stopped for a moment to consider if she had a thought. You've never cared about anyone or anything but yourself. Well, this time I won't let you without a fight. I'm going to a lawyer.

Lester.   Gert . . .

Gert.   Now get out of my house. Because brother or no, I'm through with you.

Lester.   All right. If you feel that way. (*He leaves* U.C. *of the area.* **Gert** *stands for a moment, thinking what to do next.* **Minna** *comes in* D.L. *of the area.*)

Minna.   I was behind the door and I heard the whole thing.

Gert.   Did Wilma hear?

Minna.   No, I sent her back to her room. Now you get right to a lawyer.

Gert.   I intend to. He's gotten me mad now. I won't let him get by with it if I can help it. I think I'll walk over to Bill's. I don't like to talk about it over the telephone.

Minna.   Yes'm.

Gert.   You tell Wilma to wait here for me.

Minna.   Yes'm. Want me to tell her where you've gone?

Gert.   I don't see why not. I'll be back as soon as I finish.

Minna.   Yes'm. (**Gert** *leaves* U.C. *of the area.* **Minna** *goes to the door and calls:*) Wilma. Wilma. You can come here now. (*She fills a plate with food and puts it on the table.* **Wilma** *comes in* D.L. *of the area.*) You better sit down and try to eat something.

Wilma.   I can't eat a thing.

Minna.   Well, you can try.

Wilma.   No. It would choke me. What happened?

Minna.   Your aunt told him not to sell the house, and he said he would, and so she's gone to see a lawyer.

Wilma.   Does she think she can stop him?

Minna.   She's gonna try. I know she's got him scared. . . .

Wilma.   But it's my house. You know that. He knows that. . . . Didn't she tell him?

Minna.   Sure she told him. But you know your daddy. Telling won't do any good, we have to prove it.

Wilma.   What proof have we got?

Minna.   Miss Gert's word. I hope that's enough. . . .

Wilma.   And if it isn't?

Minna.   Then you'll lose it. That's all. You'll lose it.

Wilma.   I bet I lose it. I've got no luck.

Minna.   Why do you say that?

Wilma.   What kind of luck is it takes your mama away, and then your daddy, and then tries to take your house. Sitting in that yard swinging I was the happiest girl in the world this afternoon. I'd decided not to go in the movies and to stay in Harrison and get married and have children and live in my house. . . .

Minna.   Well, losing a house won't stop you from staying in Harrison and getting married. . . .

Wilma.   Oh, yes. I wouldn't trust it with my luck. With my kind of luck I wouldn't even get me a husband. . . . I'd wind up like Miss Martha working at the post office chasing Mr. Russell Walter until the end of time. No mother and no father and no house and no husband and no children. No, thank you. I'm just tired of worrying over the whole thing. I'll just go on into Houston and see Mr.

Delafonte and get on out to Hollywood and make money and get rich and famous. *(She begins to cry.)*

Minna.   Now, honey. Honey . . .

Wilma.   Minna, I don't want to be rich and famous. . . . I want to stay here. I want to stay in Harrison. . . .

Minna.   Now, honey. Try to be brave.

Wilma.   I know what I'm gonna do. *(She jumps up.)* I'm going to see old lady Leighton. She's the one that can stop this. . . .

Minna.   Now, Wilma. You know your aunt don't want you around that woman.

Wilma.   I can't help it. I'm going. . . .

Minna.   Wilma . . . you listen to me . . . (**Wilma** *runs out* U.C. *of the area.)* Wilma . . . Wilma . . . you come back here. . . . *(But* **Wilma** *has gone.* **Minna** *shakes her head in desperation. The lights fade. . . .*

. . . When the lights are brought up it is two hours later. **Minna** *is at the kitchen table reading the paper.* **Gert** *comes in* U.C. *of the area.)*

Gert.   Well, we've won.

Minna.   What do you mean?

Gert.   I mean just what I say. Lester is not going to sell the house.

Minna.   What happened?

Gert.   I don't know what happened. I went over to see Bill and we talked it all through, and he said legally we really had no chance but he'd call up Lester and try to at least bluff him into thinking we had. And when he called Lester he said Lester wasn't home, and so I suggested his calling you know where.

Minna.   No. Where?

Gert.   Mrs. Leighton's. And sure enough he was there, and then Bill told him why he was calling and Lester said well, it didn't matter as he'd decided not to sell the house after all.

Minna. You don't mean it?

Gert. Oh, yes, I do. Where's Wilma?

Minna. She's over there with them.

Gert. Over where with them?

Minna. At Mrs. Leighton's.

Gert. Why, Minna . . .

Minna. Now don't holler at me. I told her not to go, but she said she was going and then she ran out that door so fast I couldn't stop her. (**Wilma** *comes running in* U.C. *of the area.*)

Wilma. Heard the news? House is mine again.

Minna. Do you know what happened?

Wilma. Sure. Mrs. Leighton isn't so bad. Boy, I went running over there expecting the worst . . .

Gert. Wilma, what do you mean going to that woman's house? Wilma, I declare . . .

Wilma. Oh, she's not so bad. Anyway we've got her to thank for it.

Minna. Well, what happened? Will somebody please tell me what happened?

Wilma. Well, you know I was sitting here and it came to me. It came to me just like that. See Mrs. Leighton. She's the one to stop it and it's got to be stopped. Well, I was so scared my knees were trembling the whole time going over there, but I made myself do it, walked in on her and she looked more nervous than I did.

Gert. Was your father there?

Wilma. No ma'm. He came later. Wasn't anybody there but me and Mrs. Leighton. I'm calling her Sibyl now. She asked me to. Did Arabella come yet?

Minna.   Arabella?

Wilma.   I called and asked her to come and celebrate. I'm so excited. I just had to have company tonight. I know I won't be able to sleep anyway. I hope you don't mind, Aunt Gert. . . .

Minna.   If you don't tell me what happened . . .

Wilma.   Well . . . Mrs. Leighton . . . I mean Sibyl . . . (**Arabella** *comes in* U.C. *of the area.* **Wilma** *sees her.*) Oh, come on in, Arabella.

Arabella.   Hi. I almost didn't get to come. I told my mama it was life or death and so she gave in. But she made me swear we'd be in bed by ten. Did you hear about Mr. Delafonte?

Wilma.   No? What?

Arabella.   He's a crook. It was in the Houston papers tonight. He was operating a business under false pretenses. He had been charging twenty-five dollars for those screen tests and using a camera with no film in it.

Wilma.   My goodness.

Arabella.   It was in all the papers. On the second page. My father said he mustn't have been very much not to even get on the front page. He wasn't a Hollywood director at all. He didn't even know Lila Lee or Betty Compson.

Wilma.   He didn't?

Arabella.   No.

Minna.   Wilma, will you get back to your story before I lose my mind?

Wilma.   Oh. Yes . . . I got my house back, Arabella.

Arabella.   You did?

Wilma.   Sure. That's why I called you over to spend the night. A kind of celebration.

Arabella.   Well, that's wonderful.

Minna.   Wilma . . .

Wilma.　All right. Where was I?

Gert.　You were at Mrs. Leighton's.

Wilma.　Oh, yes. Sibyl's. I'm calling her Sibyl now, Arabella. She asked me to.

Minna.　Well . . . what happened? Wilma, if you don't tell me . . .

Wilma.　Well, I just told her the whole thing.

Minna.　What whole thing?

Wilma.　Well, I told her about my mother meaning for the house to always be mine, and how I loved the house, and how I was lonely and the house was lonely and that I had hoped my daddy and I could go there and live someday but knew now we couldn't, and that I had planned to go to Hollywood and be a movie star but that this afternoon my friend Arabella and I decided we didn't really want to do that, and that I knew then that what I wanted to do really was to live in Harrison and get married and live in my house and have children so that I wouldn't be lonely any-more and the house wouldn't. And then she started crying.

Gert.　You don't mean it.

Wilma.　Yes ma'm. And I felt real sorry for her and I said I didn't hold anything against her and then Daddy came in, and she said why didn't he tell her that was my house, and he said because it wasn't. And then she asked him about what Mother told you, and he said that was true but now I was going to have a better house, and she said I didn't want to have a better house, but my own house, and that she wouldn't marry him if he sold this house and she said they both had jobs in Houston and would manage some-how, but I had nothing, so then he said all right.

Gert.　Well. Good for her.

Minna.　Sure enough, good for her.

Wilma.　And then Mr. Bill called and Daddy told him the house was mine again and then she cried again and

hugged me and asked me to kiss her and I did, and then
Daddy cried and I kissed him, and then I cried. And
they asked me to the wedding and I said I'd go and that
I'd come visit them this summer in Houston. And then I
came home.

Minna.   Well. Well, indeed.

Gert.   My goodness. So that's how it happened. And you
say Mrs. Leighton cried?

Wilma.   Twice. We all did. Daddy and Mrs. Leighton and
me. . . .

Gert.   Well, I'm glad, Wilma, it's all worked out.

Wilma.   And can I go visit them this summer in Houston?

Gert.   If you like.

Wilma.   And can I go to the wedding?

Gert.   Yes, if you want to.

Wilma.   I want to.

Minna.   Now you better have some supper.

Wilma.   No. I couldn't eat, I'm still too excited.

Minna.   Miss Gert, she hasn't had a bite on her stomach.

Gert.   Well, it won't kill her this one time, Minna.

Wilma.   Aunt Gert, can Arabella and I go over to my
yard for just a few minutes and swing? We'll be home
by ten. . . .

Gert.   No, Wilma, it's late.

Wilma.   Please. Just to celebrate. I have it coming to me.
We'll just stay for a few minutes.

Gert.   Well . . .

Wilma.   Please . . .

Gert.   Will you be back here by ten, and not make me have
to send Minna over there?

Wilma.   Yes ma'm.

Gert.　All right.

Wilma.　Oh, thank you. *(She goes to her aunt and kisses her.)* You're the best aunt in the whole world. Come on, Arabella.

Arabella.　All right. *(They start U.C. of the area.* **Gert** *calls after them:)*

Gert.　Now remember. Back by ten. Arabella has promised her mother. And you've promised me.

Wilma.　*(calling in distance)* Yes ma'm. (**Gert** *comes back into the room.)*

Gert.　Well, I'm glad it's ending this way.

Minna.　Yes ma'm.

Gert.　I never thought it would. Well, I said hard things to Lester. I'm sorry I had to, but I felt I had to.

Minna.　Of course you did.

Gert.　Well, I'll go to my room. You go on when you're ready.

Minna.　All right. I'm ready now. The excitement has wore me out.

Gert.　Me too. Leave the light on for the children. I'll keep awake until they come in.

Minna.　Yes'm.

Gert.　Good night.

Minna.　Good night. (**Gert** *goes out D.L. of the area.* **Minna** *goes to get her hat. The lights fade. The lights are brought up in the D.R. area.* **Wilma** *and* **Arabella** *come in U.C. of the area and get in the swing.)*

Wilma.　Don't you just love to swing?

Arabella.　Uh huh.

Wilma.　It's a lovely night, isn't it? Listen to that mocking-bird. The crazy thing must think it's daytime.

Arabella.　It's light enough to be day.

Wilma.   It certainly is.

Arabella.   Well, it was lucky we decided to give up Hollywood with Mr. Delafonte turning out to be a crook and all.

Wilma.   Wasn't it lucky?

Arabella.   Do you feel lonely now?

Wilma.   No, I don't feel nearly so lonely. Now I've got my house and plan to get married. And my daddy and I are going to see each other, and I think Mrs. Leighton is going to make a nice friend. She's crazy about moving pictures.

Arabella.   Funny how things work out.

Wilma.   Very funny.

Arabella.   Guess who called me on the telephone.

Wilma.   Who?

Arabella.   Tommy . . . Murray.

Wilma.   You don't say.

Arabella.   He asked me for a date next week. Picture show. He said Jay was going to call you.

Wilma.   Did he?

Arabella.   I asked him to tell Jay that you weren't only interested in going out with movie actors.

Wilma.   What did he say?

Arabella.   He said he thought Jay knew that. (*A pause.* **Wilma** *jumps out of the swing.*) Wilma.   What's the matter with you? Wilma . . . (*She runs to her.*)

Wilma.   I don't know. I felt funny there for a minute. A cloud passed over the moon and I felt lonely . . . and funny . . . and scared. . . .

Arabella.   But you have your house now.

Wilma.   I know . . . I . . . (*A pause. She points offstage* R.) I used to sleep in there. I had a white iron bed. I remember one night Aunt Gert woke me up. It was just turning light out, she was crying. "I'm taking you home to live with me," she said. "Why?" I said. "Because your mama's gone to heaven," she said. *(a pause)* I can't remember my mama's face anymore. I can hear her voice sometimes calling me far off: "Wilma, Wilma, come home." Far off. But I can't remember her face. I try and I try, but finally I have to go to my bureau drawer and take out her picture and look to remember. . . . Oh, Arabella. It isn't only the house I wanted. It's the life in the house. My mama and me and even my daddy coming in at four in the morning. . . .

Arabella.   But there'll be life again in this house.

Wilma.   How?

Arabella.   You're gonna fill it with life again, Wilma.   Like you said this afternoon.

Wilma.   But I get afraid.

Arabella.   Don't be. You will. I know you will.

Wilma.   You think I can do anything. Be a movie star. . . . Go to Hollywood. *(a pause)* The moon's from behind the cloud. *(A pause. In the distance we can hear the courthouse clock strike ten.)* Don't tell me it's ten o'clock already. I'll fill this house with life again. I'll meet a young man with steady ways and nice habits. . . . *(Far off* **Aunt Gert** *calls:* "Wilma. Wilma." **Wilma** *calls back:)* We're coming. You see that pecan tree out there?

Arabella.   Uh huh.

Wilma.   It was planted the year my mother was born. It's so big now, I can hardly reach around it. *(***Aunt Gert** *calls again:* "Wilma. Wilma." **Wilma** *calls back:)* We're coming. *(She and* **Arabella** *sit swinging. Wilma looks happy and is happy as the lights fade.)*

REVIEWING AND INTERPRETING

Record your answers to these questions in your personal literature notebook. Follow the directions for each part.

REVIEWING Try to complete each of these sentences without looking back at the play.

Recalling Facts **1.** Years earlier, whenever Wilma found her mother swinging at night, she would
   a. beg her to come back inside.
   b. ignore her and go back to bed.
   c. join her on the swing.
   d. make fun of her.

Identifying Cause and Effect **2.** Arabella doesn't want to go to Hollywood because
   a. she is afraid to speak before strangers.
   b. her parents won't give her permission to go.
   c. she doesn't trust Mr. Delafonte.
   d. she doesn't have enough money for the trip.

Identifying Sequence **3.** Wilma leaves Arabella on the swing and runs home right after
   a. a strange man asks if the house is for sale.
   b. Wilma decides she wants to live in her house with a husband.
   c. Arabella admits that she doesn't want to be a movie star.
   d. Arabella tells her that her father is planning to sell her house.

Understanding Main Ideas **4.** The house is important to Wilma because
   a. she plans on remodeling it in a few years.
   b. it reminds her of her mother and the love she felt there.
   c. she needs the rental money that it brings in.
   d. it is her only connection to her father.

Recognizing Literary
Elements (Conflict)

5. The main conflict, or problem, in this play is between
    a. Wilma and Arabella.
    b. Lester and Arabella.
    c. Wilma and Lester.
    d. Aunt Gert and Minna.

INTERPRETING

To complete these sentences, you may look back at the play if you'd like.

Making Inferences

6. The fact that Lester is slow to tell Wilma about his upcoming marriage probably means that
    a. his wife-to-be doesn't want Wilma at the wedding.
    b. he doesn't think she will be happy about it.
    c. he doesn't live in the same town as Wilma.
    d. he is a very busy man and can't find the time.

Analyzing

7. Gert sends Wilma out of the room when Lester arrives because
    a. it is time for Wilma to do her homework.
    b. she doesn't want Wilma to hear her congratulate him.
    c. she doesn't want Wilma to hear them argue.
    d. Wilma is too upset to be quiet.

Predicting Outcomes

8. The least likely outcome of the play is that Wilma will
    a. make peace with her father and stay in Harrison.
    b. get to keep her house.
    c. remain angry with her father and eventually move away.
    d. decide to go to Hollywood and will become a big movie star.

Making
Generalizations

9. One of the most important messages that readers can get from this play is that
   a. our actions affect the lives of those around us.
   b. becoming a movie star is not for everyone.
   c. an important life goal for everyone is to own property.
   d. it is best to live a normal life and not take unnecessary chances.

Understanding the
Elements of a Play
(Dialogue)

10. The characters in this play speak in a way that can be described as
   a. poetic.
   b. confusing.
   c. formal and proper.
   d. natural, like a normal conversation.

Now check your answers with your teacher. Study the questions you answered incorrectly. What types of questions were they? Talk with your teacher about ways to work on those skills.

How to Read a Play

The play is an ancient form of literature. Through the ages, people have enjoyed taking the roles of characters and acting out stories before audiences. The earliest plays may have begun as ways to honor heroes by reenacting their great deeds. They also may have started as simple entertainment around a campfire. Unfortunately, these early plays were not written down, so they are lost to us.

The ancient Greeks were among the first people to begin recording their plays. They were so enthusiastic about plays that they had drama competitions and built large theaters where crowds of up to 14,000 people could be seated to watch the performances. Greek plays have influenced Western drama ever since the sixth century B.C.

A play is a literary work that tells a story using the words and actions of characters. When playwrights write plays they expect them to be performed in front of an audience, so they include stage directions that give the performers important information. Unlike a novel or a short story, a play uses only dialogue and actions to advance the plot. It cannot use long descriptions of people, places, or feelings to let audiences know what is happening. For that reason, a play script includes only the most important words and actions.

In this unit, you will look at the ways in which playwright Horton Foote helps readers and performers understand what should be happening on the stage:

1. He uses a special format to introduce the characters and setting and to present the dialogue.

2. Throughout the play, he describes the stage and the movements of the actors upon the stage.

3. He describes the way the characters speak and the actions that they take.

LESSON 1 | THE FORMAT OF A PLAY

You probably have been reading fictional stories since you were young. So by now, you know what to expect when you pick up a short story or novel. You recognize the familiar page filled with paragraphs describing people and events. You expect to see direct quotes from the characters in the story. The form of the story itself usually gives you few surprises. On the other hand, the minute you pick up a play you recognize that you are dealing with a different—and possibly unfamiliar—kind of literature.

The first difference you'll see is that a play begins with a list of characters. This list, which is also called the *cast of characters*, is important for both performers and readers. It lets anyone who wants to perform the play know at a glance how many characters are in it, whether they are male or female, and sometimes—if descriptions are included—how old they are and what they look like. Readers can use the cast list to become familiar with the names of the characters in the play. They also can refer to it if they come upon a name they don't recognize while they read.

Some playwrights don't describe the characters in the cast list. Instead they wait until each character first appears on stage to tell about him or her. What mental picture does the playwright give you when he introduces Wilma and Arabella?

Wilma Thompson *is a handsome girl with style and spirit about her.*
Arabella Cookenboo *is gentle looking, so shy about growing into womanhood that one can't really tell yet what she is to look like or become. She is Wilma's shadow and obviously her adoring slave.*

After the characters are introduced, the setting is often described next. In *A Young Lady of Property*, the setting is clearly labeled:

Place: *Harrison, Texas*
Time: *Late spring, 1925*

Next comes a description of what the audience should see as the curtain rises. Often, the playwright is very specific about the scenery, props, and lighting. *Scenery* is the background on the stage that lets you know where the play takes place—for example, the country, the city, or a kitchen.

Props are the items that the actors use to make the play more realistic. A tree, a hat, and a kitchen stove are all examples of props. Together, the scenery and props are often called the *set*. Playwrights give directions about lighting so directors can shine lights on the most important people or action at any given time.

Try to picture the stage that the audience sees at the beginning of *A Young Lady of Property*. (L. *of* C. is the area to the left of center stage, from the actor's point of view—that is, looking out at the audience. R. *of* C. refers to the area to the right of center, and U.C. stands for Upstage Center. You will learn more about stage positions in the next lesson.)

The stage is divided into four areas. Area one, directly across the front of the stage, is a sidewalk. Area two, just above the sidewalk L. of C., *is part of a kitchen. A table, with a portable phonograph on it, and four chairs are placed here. Area three is above the sidewalk* R. of C. *It has a yard swing in it. Area four is directly* U.C. *In it is a post office window.*

Taken together, all the special instructions that the playwright provides are called *stage directions*. Stage directions let the actors and the director know what the audience should see. They also help readers picture what should be happening on stage.

Another difference between novels and plays is the way they are divided. Novels are divided into smaller sections called *chapters*. Long plays are often divided into smaller sections called *acts*. Many of the plays you will read in this book are so short that they have only one act. Some acts are further divided into *scenes*. Whenever the time or the place changes, a new scene begins. In some plays, the scenes are clearly set apart, while in others the separation between scenes is not as obvious.

Perhaps the most important difference between a play and a novel is the way the characters' words are printed. In a play, readers and performers need to know immediately who is saying the words, so the speaker's name is printed first, in a different typeface from the dialogue:

Wilma.   Heh, Arabella. Come sit and swing.
Arabella.   All right. Your letter came.
Wilma.   Whoopee. Where is it?

Reading a play is different from reading other kinds of literature. To enjoy a play, you have to be a careful reader, paying close attention to the stage directions and to which character is speaking. In addition, you have to use your imagination. Since you are not seeing the play as it was meant to be performed, you have to "fill in the blanks" by yourself. Playwrights do their best to bring their plays to life. As a reader, you must also do your part.

EXERCISE 1

Read the passage from the play on the following page. Use what you have learned in this lesson to answer the questions.

Arabella.　Wilma . . . Wilma . . . Please . . . don't say I said it. . . . Wilma . . . *(She is standing alone and frightened as the lights fade. The lights are brought up in the area* L. *of* C. **Minna** *is mixing some dough on the table.* **Miss Gert** *comes in.)*

1. Who is speaking before the scene changes?

2. How does the playwright indicate a change in scene? Where does this new scene take place?

3. If you were in charge of the props for this scene, what items would you include? Take into account the year in which the play takes place.

Now check your answers with your teacher. Review this part of the lesson if you don't understand why an answer was incorrect.

 WRITING ON YOUR OWN 1

In this exercise you will use what you have learned so far to describe a scene. Follow these steps:

- Imagine you are writing a play about what has happened to you so far today. Choose a particular event to turn into a single scene.
- Think about who will appear in your scene and write a cast of characters. You can include a short description of each person if you wish.
- Where does your scene take place? Write a short description of the scenery you would use. Also list the props you would choose to make the scene seem realistic.

LESSON 2　THE STAGE

When you are part of the audience at a play, you probably don't think much about where the actors and actresses stand on stage. If the play is done well, the performers' movements seem natural and unrehearsed. In reality, however, each character's movements are planned well in advance. When a playwright creates a play, he or she gives instructions about where each character should enter the stage, where and how the character should move while on stage, and where the character should exit. The play is like a complicated dance, and if one actor steps in the wrong direction, this can throw off the timing of the other actors.

All playwrights, directors, and actors use the same diagram of a stage. Take a few moments to study the diagram below. The entire stage is divided into nine areas. The areas are labeled from the perspective of the actors, not from the perspective of the audience. Therefore, *upstage* is the area farthest away from the audience, and *downstage* is the area closest to the audience. At the very center is *center stage*. Take special note of the abbreviations for the various parts of the stage, for example, D.R. for *Downstage Right* and U.L. for *Upstage Left*.

	Upstage Right (U.R.)	Upstage Center (U.C.)	Upstage Left (U.L.)	
Wings (Offstage Right)	Right of Center (R. of C.)	Center (C.)	Left of Center (L. of C.)	Wings (Offstage Left)
	Downstage Right (D.R.)	Downstage Center (D.C.)	Downstage Left (D.L.)	

Audience

Now look at the stage directions for one scene from *A Young Lady of Property*. Begin on page 6, as Arabella joins Wilma in the yard of her house. Stop on page 12 as the scene ends with Wilma running out of the yard and the lights fading. Notice where each actor enters and exits the stage. Compare what you pictured with the following diagram, which shows where the actors enter and exit. Did you picture their movements correctly?

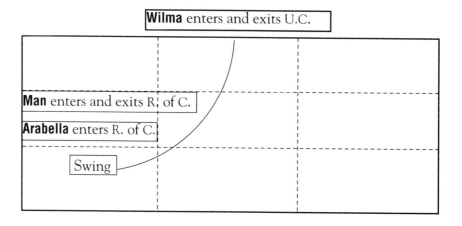

EXERCISE 2

Read this passage. Then use what you have learned in this lesson to answer the questions that follow.

> **Gert.**   All right. I will. I'll go talk to Bill. I'll find out what we can do legally. (*She starts out D.L. of the area.* **Lester** *comes in U.C. of the area.* **Minna** *sees him coming.*)
> **Minna.**   Miss Gert. (**Gert** *turns and sees him just as he gets inside the area.*)
> **Lester.**   Hello, Gert.
> **Gert.**   Hello, Lester.
> **Lester.**   Hello, Wilma.
> **Wilma.**   Hello . . .
> **Gert.**   Wilma, I think you'd better leave. . . .

Wilma. Yes'm. . . . (*She starts out.*)

Lester. Wait a minute, Gert. I've something to tell you all. I want Wilma to hear. . . .

Gert. I think we know already. Go on, Wilma.

Wilma. Yes'm. (**Wilma** leaves D.L. *of the area.* **Minna** *follows after her. A pause.*)

1. Which character enters during this passage? Which characters exit? Which character is about to exit but stops?

2. Draw a rectangle to represent the stage. Then mark where each character enters or exits.

Now check your answers with your teacher. Review this part of the lesson if you don't understand why an answer was incorrect.

WRITING ON YOUR OWN 2

In this exercise you will use what you have learned in this lesson to describe a playground and map it for the stage. Follow these steps:

- Picture a playground area that has several different pieces of equipment—swings, slides, climbing bars, a seesaw, a merry-go-round, and so on.
- Write a description of the playground as if it were on a stage. Tell what is in each of the nine stage areas. (Use the diagram on page 35 if you need help remembering the areas.) Keep in mind that stage directions are written from the actors' point of view.
- Using your stage directions as a guide, draw a diagram of the playground as it would appear on stage. In each area, write the name of the piece of equipment that you placed there in your description. Give your diagram to a classmate to check against your written description.

LESSON 3   STAGE DIRECTIONS

Almost all plays are built on dialogue. The words of the actors must convey the meaning of the play to the audience. It stands to reason that if audiences understand each word in a sentence, they will understand what the speaker is saying, right? Unfortunately, words alone do not always express the full meaning. For example, consider this simple sentence: "I know the answer." Its meaning may change, depending on how the sentence is spoken. If this sentence appears in a play, the playwright might use stage directions to tell the actor how to say the sentence so that its meaning is as clear as possible. Notice how the stage directions in the following examples change the meaning of the sentence:

> **Peter.**   (*excitedly*) I know the answer!
> **Peter.**   (*sadly*) I know the answer.
> **Peter.**   (*uncertainly*) I know the answer?
> **Peter.**   (*angrily*) I know the answer.

When people talk, they use their bodies as well as their voices to express themselves. Sometimes they use hand gestures to illustrate or emphasize what they are saying. Sometimes they show their true feelings by the way they move around a room or stand close to or far from other people in the room. Playwrights are aware of how important body language is in helping to convey meaning. That's why they include stage directions that provide instructions for movements and expressions. Look at the way playwright Horton Foote describes how Wilma opens the letter from the Hollywood agent:

> **Arabella.**   Here. (*She gives it to her.* **Wilma** *tears it open.* . . .)

Wilma *tears* open the letter eagerly. She doesn't open it carefully with a letter opener or put it aside to open it later.

The stage direction lets the reader know Wilma's state of mind and tells the actor how to perform the action correctly.

EXERCISE 3

Read this passage in which Wilma accepts Arabella's decision not to go to Hollywood. Then use what you have learned in this lesson to answer the questions that follow the passage.

> **Wilma.** I'll go in a little. I love to swing in my front yard. . . . (*A pause. She looks out into the yard.*) The pear tree looks sickly, doesn't it? The fig trees are doing nicely though. I was out in back and the weeds are near knee high, but fig trees just seem to thrive in the weeds. The freeze must have killed off the banana trees. . . . (*A pause.* **Wilma** *stops swinging—she walks around the yard.*) Maybe I won't leave either. Maybe I won't go to Hollywood after all. . . .
>
> **Arabella.** Oh, Wilma. Don't go to Hollywood. Stay here in Harrison and let's be friends forever. . . .
> **Wilma.** All right. I will.
> **Arabella.** You will?
> **Wilma.** Sure, why not? I'll stay here. I'll stay here and marry and live in my house.
> **Arabella.** Oh, Wilma. I'm so glad. I'm so very glad. (**Wilma** *gets back in the swing. They swing vigorously back and forth. . . .*)

1. Wilma has just heard that her best friend is backing out of their exciting plan, leaving her alone in the adventure. Why do you think the playwright has Wilma get off the swing and start walking around the yard at this point? How are her actions connected to her next words?

2. What emotions do you think are emphasized by the stage direction that describes Wilma and Arabella as swinging "vigorously back and forth"?

Now check your answers with your teacher. Review this part of the lesson if you don't understand why an answer was incorrect.

 WRITING ON YOUR OWN 3

In this exercise you will add stage directions to a simple dialogue. Follow these steps:

• Read this dialogue:

Derrick. Here. The telephone's for you.
Gina. Thanks. . . . Hello? . . . Hi. . . . Sure. What time? . . . Sounds good! See you later.
Derrick. What was that all about? I thought you were going to study tonight.
Gina. No. I'm all caught up at school and this movie is supposed to be good. I'll be back early.
Derrick. It's your life.

• Now rewrite the dialogue. Add stage directions that tell how the actors should say the words. After each character's name, write the stage directions in parentheses and underline them to set them apart. For example, you might add *(sarcastically)* before Derrick's final line.
• Rewrite the dialogue again, this time adding stage directions to describe the actors' facial expressions and movements. For example, you might add *(grabbing the phone out of his hand)* before Gina's first line.

DISCUSSION GUIDES

1. It is made clear in the play that the family home is in Wilma's father's name. He has the legal right to sell it if he wants to. However, he promised Wilma's mother while she was on her deathbed that he would give the home to Wilma. Do you think he has the moral right to sell the home? Discuss the problem with a small group of classmates. Come to a group decision and then share your decision with the rest of the class. (If you can't all come to the same decision, form two separate groups.) Be ready to present your arguments in a class discussion.

2. Arabella's mother advises her that the normal life for a girl is to marry and have children, not to move away and become an actress. This play is set in 1925, when most people would have said that daughters should stay close to home and live traditional lives. Do you think a mother would give her daughter the same advice if the play were set in the present time? If so, why? If not, how would the advice be different? Work with a partner to write a dialogue that could take place between a parent and a child today. Have the characters discuss the child's future goals. The child should be explaining his or her plans and desires, and the parent should be giving the child advice. Practice performing the dialogue, and then present it to the class.

3. For many reasons, Wilma's relationship with her father is not good. Wilma and her father would probably like to get along better but are not sure how to improve the situation. Work with a small group to make a "how-to" guide for parents and children like Lester and Wilma. First list what you feel children have a right to expect from their parents. Then list what parents should expect from their children. Share your guide with the rest of the class. Look for the similarities and differences among the guides.

WRITE A SCENE

In this unit, you have seen how playwrights use stage directions to help directors, actors, and readers understand their plays. Now you will write an original scene using stage directions.

Follow these steps to complete your scene. If you have questions about the writing process, refer to Using the Writing Process (page 261).

- Assemble the following writing assignments, which you completed in this unit: 1) a diagram of a scene from a remembered play; 2) a description of a scene from a play about an event in your life; 3) a description of a playground setting, along with a diagram showing stage positions for equipment; 4) a simple dialogue with added stage directions.

- Look over these assignments for ideas for writing your own scene. Then choose a setting for the scene you will write. Jot down notes describing what the audience should see as the curtain rises.

- Decide on the characters who will appear in the scene. If you'd like, the scene can be taken from your life or from the life of someone you know.

- Begin by listing the cast of characters who will appear in the scene. Describe each character briefly. Then describe the setting, complete with the scenery and props that you feel would be right for your scene.

- Next, write a short dialogue between or among the people in your scene. Be sure to include stage directions in parentheses. The stage directions should tell the actors how to speak the words and how to move around the stage.

- Proofread your scene for spelling, grammar, punctuation, and capitalization errors. Then make a final copy.

- Ask some classmates to help you perform the scene. Get help from your teacher, if necessary, and make a copy for each person in the scene. Rehearse the scene a few times and then act it out for the rest of the class. After you have finished, put a copy of the scene in your writing portfolio.

Plot

Back There

by Rod Serling

INTRODUCTION

ABOUT THE SELECTION

Is time travel possible? If it is possible, can a time traveler make a difference in history? Author Rod Serling explores these questions in his television play *Back There*. As the play begins, Peter Corrigan is discussing the possibility of time travel with his friends at the Washington Club. Soon after he insists that time travel is impossible, he finds himself transported to an April day in 1865. The play describes how Corrigan tries to change the outcome of an important historical event.

ABOUT THE AUTHOR

Rod Serling (1924–1975) was born in Syracuse, New York. He wrote his first plays for the radio but soon switched to writing for an exciting new medium—television. Early in his career, his teleplay *Requiem for a Heavyweight* earned him an Emmy award. Serling would eventually earn six Emmys for his television writing. Three of those awards were for episodes from his popular TV series, *The Twilight Zone*. Serling was creator, host, and head writer for the series, which aired from 1959 to 1965. Audiences tuned in every week to be entertained, frightened, and thrilled by his science fiction and fantasy stories.

The selection you are about to read is an episode from *The Twilight Zone*. Although both this series and his later series *Night Gallery* were considered entertainment, they raised serious questions about human nature and modern society. In addition to his television scripts, Serling is known for his screenplay work—he was a cowriter for the science-fiction movie *Planet of the Apes*.

ABOUT THE LESSONS

The lessons that follow *Back There* focus on the plot in a play. You know that a play tells a story through the words and actions of the actors. Like any other story, a play must have a *plot*—an overall plan of story events. Most plots follow a familiar pattern. First, the author introduces the setting and the characters. Next, the author introduces the *conflict*, or problem, that the characters face. The problem grows until a turning point, or *climax*, is reached. Finally, the action falls as the problem is solved, and the story ends.

 WRITING: DEVELOPING A PLOT

At the end of this unit, you will create a storyboard for an original play. A *storyboard* is a device that writers use to create pictures of the most important events in a plot. These pictures are arranged in time order. As writers "flesh out," or fill in the details of their novel, play, or movie, they can look back at the storyboard to see if they are staying on track with their original ideas.

The following suggestions will help you begin thinking about the events in your play:

- Think of a simple, familiar story such as "The Three Little Pigs" or "Snow White."
- Take several notecards or sentence strips and write a sentence describing one important event from the story on the bottom of each card. Don't worry if some of the events are out of order at this point.
- Now arrange the notecards or strips in the order in which the events happened. Ask a classmate to look over your arrangement to see if he or she agrees with the order.
- When you have the order correct, number the backs of your cards or strips to keep them in order more easily.

AS YOU READ

Think about these questions as you read the selection. They will help you take note of how the author builds the plot.

- How does the author introduce you to the characters and the setting?
- What problem, or conflict, does the main character face?
- What is the climax, or turning point, of this selection?
- How does the author build excitement until the climax?
- How is the conflict solved?

Back There

by Rod Serling

	Corrigan, *a young skeptic[1] who learns better, and panics*
	William, *an attendant; a calm gentleman who could be either a servant or a millionaire*
	Captain of Police, *incorruptibly dense*
	Policeman, *average*
	Wellington, *tall and authoritative; cape and moustache*
	Police Officer, *young and sympathetic*
	Jackson, *clubman*
	Millard, *clubman*
	Whitaker, *clubman*
	Attendant
	Mrs. Landers, *a fussy landlady*
	Lieutenant ⎫
	His Girl ⎬ *two handsome young people*
	Landlady
	Attendant Two
	Two voices
	Narrator

---

[1] one who doubts as a matter of habit

ACT ONE

SCENE 1   *Exterior of club at night*

(Near a large front entrance of double doors is a name plaque in brass which reads "The Washington Club, Founded 1858." In the main hall of the building is a large paneled foyer with rooms leading off on either side. An attendant, **William,** *carrying a tray of drinks, crosses the hall and enters one of the rooms. There are four men sitting around in the aftermath of a card game.* **Peter Corrigan** *is the youngest, then two middle-aged men named* **Whitaker** *and* **Millard,** *and* **Jackson,** *the oldest, a white-haired man in his sixties, who motions the tray from the attendant over to the table.)*

Jackson.   Just put it over here, William, would you?

William.   Yes, sir. (*He lays the tray down and walks away from the table.*)

Corrigan.   Now what's your point? That if it were possible for a person to go back in time there'd be nothing in the world to prevent him from altering the course of history—is that it?

Millard.   Let's say, Corrigan, that you go back in time. It's October, 1929. The day before the stock market crashed. You know on the following morning that the securities are going to tumble into an abyss. Now using that prior knowledge, there's a hundred things you can do to protect yourself.

Corrigan.   But I'm an anachronism[2] back there. I don't really belong back there.

Millard.   You could sell out the day before the crash.

Corrigan.   But what if I did and that started the crash earlier? Now history tells us that on October 24th, 1929, the bottom dropped out of the stock market. That's a fixed date. October 24th, 1929. It exists as an event in the history of our times. It *can't* be altered.

---

[2] anything that exists outside its normal time

Millard. And I say it can. What's to prevent it? What's to prevent me, say, from going to a broker[3] on the morning of October 23rd?

Corrigan. Gentlemen, I'm afraid I'll have to leave this time travel to H. G. Wells. I'm much too tired to get into any more metaphysics this evening. And since nobody has ever gone back in time, the whole blamed thing is much too theoretical.[4] I'll probably see you over the weekend.

Whittaker. Don't get lost back in time now, Corrigan.

Corrigan. I certainly shall not. Good night, everybody.

Voices. Good night, Pete. Good night, Corrigan. See you tomorrow. (**Corrigan** *walks out into the hall and heads toward the front door.*)

William (the attendant). (*going by*) Good night, Mr. Corrigan.

Corrigan. Good night, William. (*Then he looks at the elderly man a little more closely.*) Everything all right with you, William? Looks like you've lost some weight.

William. (*with a deference[5] built of a forty-year habit pattern*) Just the usual worries, sir. The stars and my salary are fixed. It's the cost of living that goes up. (**Corrigan** *smiles, reaches in his pocket, starts to hand him a bill.*)

William. Oh no, sir. I couldn't.

Corrigan. (*forcing it into his hand*) Yes, you can, William. Bless you and say hello to your wife for me.

William. Thank you so much, sir. (*a pause*) Did you have a coat with you?

Corrigan. No. I'm rushing the season a little tonight, William. I felt spring in the air. Came out like this.

William. (*opening the door*) Well, April *is* spring, sir.

---

[3] one who buys and sells stocks for others

[4] based only on reasoning without proof

[5] polite repect

Corrigan.   It's getting there. What is the date, William?

William.   April 14th, sir.

Corrigan.   April 14th. (*Then he turns, grins at the attendant.*) 1965—right?

William.   I beg your pardon, sir? Oh, yes, sir. 1965.

Corrigan.   (*going out*) Good night, William. Take care of yourself. (*He goes out into the night.*)

SCENE 2   *Exterior of the club*

(*The door closes behind* **Corrigan.** *He stands there near the front entrance. The light from the street light illuminates the steps. There's the sound of chimes from the distant steeple clock.* **Corrigan** *looks at his wrist watch, holding it out toward the light so it can be seen more clearly. Suddenly his face takes on a strange look. He shuts his eyes and rubs his temple. Then he looks down at his wrist again. This time the light has changed. It's a wavery, moving light, different from what it had been.* **Corrigan** *looks across toward the light again. It's a gas light now. He reacts in amazement. The chimes begin to chime again, this time eight times. He once again looks at the watch, but instead of a wrist watch there is just a fringe of lace protruding from a coat. There is no wrist watch at all. He grabs his wrist, pulling at the lace and coat. He's dressed now in a nineteenth-century costume. He looks down at himself, looks again toward the gas light that flickers, and then slowly backs down from the steps staring at the building from which he's just come. The plaque reads "Washington Club." He jumps the steps two at a time, slams against the front door, pounding on it. After a long moment the door opens. An attendant, half undressed, stands there peering out into the darkness.*)

Attendant.   Who is it? What do you want?

Corrigan.   I left something in there. (*He starts to push his way in and the attendant partially closes the door on him.*)

Attendant.   Now here you! The Club is closed this evening.

Corrigan.   The devil it is. I just left here a minute ago.

Attendant.   (*peers at him*) You did what? You drunk, young man? That it? You're drunk, huh?

Corrigan.   I am not drunk. I want to see Mr. Jackson or Mr. Whitaker, or William. Let me talk to William. Where is he now?

Attendant.   Who?

Corrigan.   William. What's the matter with you? Where did you come from? (*Then he looks down at his clothes.*) What's the idea of this? (*He looks up. The door has been shut. He pounds on it again, shouting.*) Hey! Open up!

Voice.   (*from inside*) You best get away from here or I'll call the police. Go on. Get out of here. (**Corrigan** *backs away from the door, goes down to the sidewalk, stands there, looks up at the gas light, then up and down the street, starts at the sound of noises. It's the clip-clop of horses' hooves and the rolling, squeaky sound of carriage wheels. He takes a few halting, running steps out into the street. He bites his lip, looks around.*)

Corrigan.   (*under his breath*) I'll go home. That's it. Go home. I'll go home. (*He turns and starts to walk and then run down the street, disappearing into the night.*)

SCENE 3   *Hallway of rooming house*

(*There is the sound of a doorbell ringing.* **Mrs. Landers**, *the landlady, comes out from the dining room and goes toward the door.*)

Mrs. Landers.   All right. All right. Have a bit of patience. I'm coming.

Mrs. Landers.   (*opening door*) Yes?

Corrigan.   Is this 19 West 12th Street?

Mrs. Landers.   That's right. Whom did you wish to see?

Corrigan.   I'm just wondering if . . . (*He stands there trying to look over her shoulder.* **Mrs. Landers** *turns to look behind her and then suspiciously back toward* **Corrigan**.)

Mrs. Landers.   Whom did you wish to see, young man?

Corrigan.   I . . . I used to live here. It's the oldest building in this section of town.

Mrs. Landers.   (*stares at him*) How's that?

Corrigan.   (*wets his lips*) What I mean is . . . as I remember it . . . it was the oldest—

Mrs. Landers.   Well now really, young man. I can't spend the whole evening standing here talking about silly things like which is the oldest building in the section. Now if there's nothing else—

Corrigan.   (*blurting it out*) Do you have a room?

Mrs. Landers.   (*Opens the door just a little bit wider so that she can get a better look at him. She looks him up and down and appears satisfied.*) I have a room for acceptable boarders. Do you come from around here?

Corrigan.   Yes. Yes, I do.

Mrs. Landers.   Army veteran?

Corrigan.   Yes. Yes, as a matter of fact I am.

Mrs. Landers.   (*looks at him again up and down*) Well, come in. I'll show you what I have. (*She opens the door wider and* **Corrigan** *enters. She closes it behind him. She looks expectantly up toward his hat and* **Corrigan** *rather hurriedly and abruptly removes it. He grins, embarrassed.*)

Corrigan.   I'm not used to it.

Mrs. Landers.   Used to what?

Corrigan.   (*points to the hat in his hand*) The hat. I don't wear a hat very often.

Mrs. Landers.   (*again gives him her inventory look, very unsure of him now*) May I inquire as to what your business is?

Corrigan.   I'm an engineer.

Mrs. Landers.   Really. A professional man. Hmmm. Well, come upstairs and I'll show you. (*She points to the stairs* *that lead off the hall and* **Corrigan** *starts up as an army officer with a pretty girl comes down them.)*

Mrs. Landers.   *(smiling)* Off to the play?

Lieutenant.   That's right, Mrs. Landers. Dinner at The Willard and then off to the play.

Mrs. Landers.   Well, enjoy yourself. And applaud the President for me!

Lieutenant.   We'll certainly do that.

Girl.   Good night, Mrs. Landers.

Mrs. Landers.   Good night, my dear. Have a good time. This way, Mr. Corrigan. *(The* **Lieutenant** *and* **Corrigan** *exchange a nod as they pass on the stairs. As they go up the steps,* **Corrigan** *suddenly stops and* **Mrs. Landers** *almost bangs into him.)*

Mrs. Landers.   Now what's the trouble?

Corrigan.   *(whirling around)* What did you say?

Mrs. Landers.   What did I say to whom? When?

Corrigan.   To the lieutenant. To the officer. What did you just say to him? *(The* **Lieutenant** *has turned. The* **Girl** *tries to lead him out, but he holds out his hand to stop her so that he can listen to the conversation from the steps.)*

Corrigan.   You just said something to him about the President.

Lieutenant.   *(walking toward the foot of the steps)* She told me to applaud him. Where might your sympathies lie?

Mrs. Landers.   *(suspiciously)* Yes, young man. Which army were you in?

Corrigan.   *(wets his lips nervously)* The Army of the Republic, of course.

Lieutenant.   *(nods, satisfied)* Then why make such a thing of applauding President Lincoln? That's his due, we figure.

Mrs. Landers.   That and everything else, may the good Lord bless him.

Corrigan. *(takes a step down the stairs, staring at the* **Lieutenant***)* You're going to a play tonight? (*The* **Lieutenant** *nods.)*

Girl. *(at the door)* We may or we may not, depending on when my husband makes up his mind to get a carriage in time to have dinner and get to the theatre.

Corrigan. What theatre? *What* play?

Lieutenant. Ford's Theatre, of course.

Corrigan. *(looking off, his voice intense)* Ford's Theatre. Ford's Theatre.

Lieutenant. Are you all right? I mean do you feel all right?

Corrigan. *(whirls around to stare at him)* What's the name of the play?

Lieutenant. *(exchanges a look with his wife)* I beg your pardon?

Corrigan. The play. The one you're going to tonight at Ford's Theatre. What's the name of it?

Girl. It's called "Our American Cousin."

Corrigan. *(again looks off thoughtfully)* "Our American Cousin" and Lincoln's going to be there.

Corrigan. *(looks from one to the other, first toward the* **Landlady** *on the steps, then down toward the* **Lieutenant** *and his wife)* And it's April 14th, 1865, isn't it? Isn't it April 14th, 1865? (*He starts down the steps without waiting for an answer. The* **Lieutenant** *stands in front of him.)*

Lieutenant. Really, sir, I'd call your actions most strange. (**Corrigan** *stares at him briefly as he goes by, then goes out the door, looking purposeful and intent.)*

SCENE 4 *Alley at night*

(On one side is the stage door with a sign over it reading "Ford's Theatre." **Corrigan** *turns the corridor into the alley at a dead*

run. He stops directly under the light, looks left and right, then vaults over the railing and pounds on the stage door.)

Corrigan. *(shouting)* Hey! Hey, let me in! President Lincoln is going to be shot tonight! (*He continues to pound on the door and shout.*)

ACT TWO

SCENE 1 *Police station at night*

(*It's a bare receiving room with a police* **Captain** *at a desk. A long bench on one side of the room is occupied by sad miscreants[6] awaiting disposition. There is a line of three or four men standing in front of the desk with several policemen in evidence. One holds onto* **Corrigan** *who has a bruise over his eye and his coat is quite disheveled.[7] The police* **Captain** *looks up to him from a list.*)

Captain. Now what's this one done? (*He peers up over his glasses and eyes* **Corrigan** *up and down.*) Fancy Dan with too much money in his pockets, huh?

Corrigan. While you idiots are sitting here, you're going to lose a President! (*The* **Captain** *looks inquiringly toward the* **Policeman.***)

Policeman. That's what he's been yellin' all the way over to the station. And that's what the doorman at the Ford Theatre popped him on the head for. (*He nods toward* **Corrigan.***) Tried to pound his way right through the stage door. Yellin' some kind of crazy things about President Lincoln goin' to get shot.

Corrigan. President Lincoln *will* be shot! Tonight. In the theatre. A man named Booth.

Captain. And how would you be knowin' this? I suppose you're clairvoyant or something. Some kind of seer or wizard or something.

---

[6] one who has committed a crime

[7] messy, not tidy

Corrigan.   I only know what I know. If I told you *how* I knew, you wouldn't believe me. Look, keep me here if you like. Lock me up.

Captain.   (*motions toward a turnkey,*[8] *points to cell block door*) Let him sleep it off. (*The turnkey grabs* **Corrigan**'*s arm and starts to lead him out of the room.*)

Corrigan.   (*shouting as he's led away*) Well you boobs better hear me out. Somebody better get to the President's box at the Ford Theatre. Either keep him out of there or put a cordon of men around him. A man named John Wilkes Booth is going to assassinate him tonight! (*He's pushed through the door leading to the cell block. A tall man in cape and black moustache stands near the open door at the other side. He closes it behind him, takes a step into the room, then with a kind of very precise authority, he walks directly over to the* **Captain**'*s table, shoving a couple of people aside as he does so with a firm gentleness. When he reaches the* **Captain**'*s table he removes a card from his inside pocket, puts it on the table in front of the* **Captain**.)

Wellington.   Wellington, Captain. Jonathan Wellington. (*The* **Captain** *looks at the card, peers at it over his glasses, then looks up toward the tall man in front of him. Obviously the man's manner and dress impress him. His tone is respect-ful and quiet.*)

Captain.   What can I do for you, Mr. Wellington?

Wellington.   That man you just had incarcerated.[9] Mr. Corrigan I believe he said his name was.

Captain.   Drunk, sir. That's probably what he is.

Wellington.   Drunk or . . . (*He taps his head meaningfully.*) Or perhaps, ill. I wonder if he could be remanded in my cus-tody. He might well be a war veteran and I'd hate to see him placed in jail.

---

[8] one who keeps the jail keys

[9] put in jail

Captain.   Well, that's real decent of you, Mr. Wellington. You say you want him remanded in *your* custody?

Wellington.   Precisely. I'll be fully responsible for him. I think perhaps I might be able to help him.

Captain.   All right, sir. If that's what you'd like. But I'd be careful of this one if I was you! There's a mighty bunch of crack-pots running the streets these days and many of them his like, and many of them dangerous too, sir. (*He turns toward turnkey.*) Have Corrigan brought back out here. This gentleman's going to look after him. (*Then he turns to* **Wellington**.) It's real decent of you sir. Real decent indeed.

Wellington.   I'll be outside. Have him brought out to me if you would.

Captain.   I will indeed, sir. (**Wellington** *turns. He passes the various people who look at him and make room for him. His walk, his manner, his positiveness suggest a commanding fig-ure and everyone reacts accordingly. The* **Captain** *once again busies himself with his list and is about to check in the next prisoner, when a young* **Police Officer** *alongside says:*)

Police Officer.   Begging your pardon, Captain.

Captain.   What is it?

Police Officer.   About that Corrigan, sir.

Captain.   What about him?

Police Officer.   Wouldn't it be wise, sir, if—

Captain.   (*impatiently*) If what?

Police Officer.   He seemed so positive, sir. So sure. About the President, I mean.

Captain.   (*slams on the desk with vast impatience*) What would you have us do? Send all available police to the Ford Theatre? And on what authority? On the word of some demented fool who probably left his mind someplace in Gettysburg. If I was you, mister, I'd be considerably more thoughtful at sizing up situations or you'll not advance one half grade the next twenty years. Now be good enough to stand aside and let me get on with my work.

Police Officer.   *(very much deterred by all this, but pushed on by a gnawing sense of disquiet)* Captain, it wouldn't hurt.

Captain.   *(interrupting with a roar)* It wouldn't hurt if what?

Police Officer.   I was going to suggest, sir, that if perhaps we placed extra guards in the box with the President—

Captain.   The President has all the guards he needs. He's got the whole Federal Army at his disposal and if they're satisfied with his security arrangements, then I am too and so should you. Next case! *(The young **Police Officer** bites his lip and looks away, then stares across the room thoughtfully. The door opens and the turnkey leads **Corrigan** across the room and over to the door. He opens it and points out. **Corrigan** nods and walks outside. The door closes behind him. The young **Police Officer** looks briefly at the **Captain**, then puts his cap on and starts out toward the door.)*

SCENE 2   *Lodging-house, **Wellington**'s room*

*(**Wellington** is pouring wine into two glasses. **Corrigan** sits in a chair, his face in his hands. He looks up at the proffered drink and takes it.)*

Wellington.   Take this. It'll make you feel better. *(**Corrigan** nods his thanks, takes a healthy swig of the wine, puts it down, then looks up at the other man.)* Better?

Corrigan.   *(studying the man)* Who are you anyway?

Wellington.   *(with a thin smile)* At the moment I'm your benefactor and apparently your only friend. I'm in the Government service, but as a young man in college I dabbled in medicine of a sort.

Corrigan.   Medicine?

Wellington.   Medicine of the mind.

Corrigan. *(smiles grimly)* Psychiatrist.

Wellington. *(turning to him)* I don't know the term.

Corrigan. What about the symptoms?

Wellington. They *do* interest me. This story you were telling about the President being assassinated.

Corrigan. *(quickly)* What time *is* it?

Wellington. There's time. *(checks a pocket watch)* A quarter to eight. The play won't start for another half hour. What gave you the idea that the President would be assassinated?

Corrigan. I happen to know, that's all.

Wellington. *(again the thin smile)* You have a premonition?[10]

Corrigan. I've got a devil of a lot more than a premonition. Lincoln *will* be assassinated. *(then quickly)* Unless somebody tries to prevent it.

Wellington. *I* shall try to prevent it. If you can convince me that you're neither drunk nor insane.

Corrigan. *(on his feet)* If I told you what I was, you'd be convinced I *was* insane. So all I'm *going* to tell you is that I happen to know for a fact that a man named John Wilkes Booth will assassinate President Lincoln in his box at the Ford Theatre. I don't know what time it's going to happen . . . that's something I forgot—but—

Wellington. *(softly)* Something you forgot?

Corrigan. *(takes a step toward him)* Listen, please—(*He stops suddenly, and begins to waver. He reaches up to touch the bruise over his head.*)

Wellington. *(takes out a handkerchief and hands it to **Corrigan**)* Here. That hasn't been treated properly. You'd best cover it.

Corrigan. *(very, very shaky, almost faint, takes the handkerchief, puts it to his head and sits back down weakly)* That's . . . that's odd. (*He looks up, still holding the handkerchief.*)

---

[10]warning before the event

Wellington. What is?

Corrigan. I'm so . . . I'm so faint all of a sudden. So weak. It's almost as if I were—

Wellington. As if you were what?

Corrigan. *(with a weak smile)* As if I'd suddenly gotten drunk or some—*(He looks up, desperately trying to focus now as his vision starts to become clouded.)* I've never . . . I've never felt like this before. I've never—*(His eyes turn to the wine glass on the table. As his eyes open wide, he struggles to his feet.)* You . . . you devil! You drugged me, didn't you! *(He reaches out to grab* **Wellington**, *half struggling in the process.)* You drugged me, didn't you!

Wellington. I was forced to, my young friend. You're a very sick man and a sick man doesn't belong in jail. He belongs in a comfortable accommodation where he can sleep and rest and regain his . . . *(He smiles a little apologetically.)* his composure, his rationale. Rest, Mr. Corrigan. I'll be back soon. *(He turns and starts toward the door.* **Corrigan** *starts to follow him, stumbles to his knees, supports himself on one hand, looks up as* **Wellington** *opens the door.)*

Corrigan. Please . . . please, you've got to believe me. Lincoln's going to be shot tonight.

Wellington. *(smiling again)* And *that's* odd! Because . . . perhaps I'm *beginning* to believe you! Good night, Mr. Corrigan. Rest well. *(He turns and goes out of the room, closing the door behind him. We hear the sound of the key being inserted, the door locked.* **Corrigan** *tries desperately to rise and then weakly falls over on his side. He crawls toward the door. He scrabbles at it with a weak hand.)*

Corrigan. *(almost in a whisper)* Please . . . please . . . somebody . . . let me out. I wasn't kidding . . . I know . . . *the President's going to be assassinated!* *(His arm, supporting him, gives out and he falls to his face, then in a last effort, he turns himself over so that he's lying on his back.)*

(There is a sound of a heavy knocking on the door. Then a **Landlady**'s *voice from outside.)*

Landlady. There's no need to break it open, Officer. I've got an extra key. Now if you don't mind, stand aside. *(There's the sound of the key inserted in the lock and the door opens. The young* **Police Officer** *from earlier is standing there with an angry-faced* **Landlady** *behind him. The* **Police Officer** *gets down on his knees, props up* **Corrigan**'s *head.)*

Police Officer. Are you all right? What's happened?

Corrigan. What time is it? *(He grabs the officer, almost pulling him over.)* You've got to tell me what time it is.

Police Officer. It's ten-thirty-five. Come on, Corrigan. You've got to tell me what you know about this. You may be a madman or a drunk or I don't know what—but you've got me convinced and I've been everywhere from the Mayor's office to the Police Commissioner's home trying to get a special guard for the President.

Corrigan. Then go yourself. Find out where he's sitting and get right up alongside of him. He'll be shot from behind. That's the way it happened. Shot from behind. And then the assassin jumps from the box to the stage and he runs out of the wings.

Police Officer. *(incredulous)* You're telling me this as if, as if it has already happened.

Corrigan. It *has* happened. It happened a hundred years ago and I've come back to see that it *doesn't* happen. *(looking beyond the* **Police Officer***)* Where's the man who brought me in here? Where's Wellington?

Landlady. *(peering into the room)* Wellington? There's no one here by that name.

Corrigan. *(Waves a clenched fist at her. He still holds the hand-kerchief.)* Don't tell me there's no one here by that name. He brought me in here. He lives in this room.

Landlady. There's no one here by that name.

Corrigan. *(holds the handkerchief close to his face, again waving his fist)* I tell you the man who brought me here was named— *(He stops abruptly, suddenly caught by something he sees on the handkerchief. His eyes slowly turn to stare at it in his hand. On the border are the initials J.W.B.)*

Corrigan. J.W.B.?

Landlady. Of course! Mr. John Wilkes Booth who lives in this room and that's who brought you here.

Corrigan. He said his name was Wellington! And that's why he drugged me. *(He grabs the* **Police Officer** *again.)* He gave me wine and he drugged me. He didn't want me to stop him. He's the one who's going to do it. Listen, you've got to get to that theatre. You've got to stop him. John Wilkes Booth! He's going to kill Lincoln. Look, get out of here now! Will you stop him? Will you— *(He stops abruptly, his eyes look up. All three people turn to look toward the window. There's the sound of crowd noises building, suggestive of excitement, and then almost a collective wail, a mournful, universal chant that comes from the streets, and as the sound builds we suddenly hear intelligible words that are part of the mob noise.)*

Voices. The President's been shot. President Lincoln's been assassinated. Lincoln is dying.

(The **Landlady** *suddenly bursts into tears. The* **Police Officer** *rises to his feet, his face white.)*

Police Officer. Oh my dear God! You were right. You *did* know. Oh . . . my . . . dear . . . God! *(He turns, almost trance-like, and walks out of the room. The* **Landlady** *follows him.* **Corrigan** *rises weakly and goes to the window, staring out at the night and listening to the sounds of a nation beginning its mourning. He closes his eyes and puts his head against the windowpane and with fruitless, weakened smashes, hits the side of the window frame as he talks.)*

Corrigan. I tried to tell you. I tried to warn you. Why didn't anybody listen? Why? Why didn't anyone listen to me? (*His fist beats a steady staccato on the window frame.*)

SCENE 3   *The Washington Club at night*

(**Corrigan** *is pounding on the front door of the Washington Club.* **Corrigan** *is standing there in modern dress once again. The door opens. An attendant we've not seen before appears.*)

Attendant Two.   Good evening, Mr. Corrigan. Did you forget something, sir? (**Corrigan** *walks past the attendant, through the big double doors that lead to the card room as in Act I. His three friends are in the middle of a discussion. The fourth man at the table, sitting in his seat, has his back to the camera.*)

Millard.   (*looking up*) Hello, Pete. Come on over and join tonight's bull session. It has to do with the best ways of amassing a fortune. What are your tried-and-true methods?

Corrigan.   (*His voice is intense and shaky.*) We were talking about time travel, about going back in time.

Jackson.   (*dismissing it*) Oh that's old stuff. We're on a new tack now. Money and the best ways to acquire it.

Corrigan.   Listen . . . listen, I want to tell you something. This is true. If you go back into the past you can't change anything. (*He takes another step toward the table.*) Understand? You can't change anything. (*The men look at one another, disarmed by the intensity of* **Corrigan**'s *tone.*)

Jackson.   (*rises, softly*) All right, old man, if you say so. (*studying him intensely*) Are you all right?

Corrigan.   (*closing his eyes for a moment*) Yes . . . yes, I'm all right.

Jackson.   Then come on over and listen to a lot of palaver[11] from self-made swindlers.[12] William here has the best method.

---

[11] useless chatter

[12] one who cheats another to get money

Corrigan. William? (*He sees the attendant from Act I but now meticulously dressed, a middle-aged millionaire obviously, with a totally different manner, who puts a cigarette in a holder with manicured hands in the manner of a man totally accustomed to wealth.* **William** *looks up and smiles.*)

William. Oh yes. My method for achieving security is far the best. You simply inherit it. It comes to you in a beribboned box. I was telling the boys here, Corrigan. My great grandfather was on the police force here in Washington on the night of Lincoln's assassination. He went all over town trying to warn people that something might happen. (*He holds up his hands in a gesture.*) How he figured it out, nobody seems to know. It's certainly not recorded any place. But because there was so much publicity, people never forgot him. He became a police chief, then a councilman, did some wheeling and dealing in land and became a millionaire. What do you say we get back to our bridge, gentlemen? (**Jackson** *takes the cards and starts to shuffle.* **William** *turns in his seat once again.*)

William. How about it, Corrigan? Take a hand?

Corrigan. Thank you, William, no. I think I'll . . . I think I'll just go home. (*He turns very slowly and starts toward the exit. Over his walk we hear the whispered, hushed murmurings of the men at the table.*)

Voices. Looks peaked, doesn't he? Acting so strangely. I wonder what's the matter with him.

(**Corrigan** *walks into the hall and toward the front door.*)

Narrator's Voice. Mr. Peter Corrigan, lately returned from a place "Back There"; a journey into time with highly questionable results. Proving, on one hand, that the threads of history are woven tightly and the skein of events cannot be undone; but, on the other hand, there are small fragments of tapestry that *can* be altered. Tonight's thesis, to be taken as you will, in *The Twilight Zone!*

REVIEWING AND INTERPRETING

Record your answers to these questions in your personal literature notebook. Follow the directions for each part.

REVIEWING

Try to complete each of these sentences without looking back at the play.

Identifying Sequence

1. The first thing that Corrigan does after leaving his friends at the Washington Club is
   a. notice that his clothes have changed.
   b. look at his wrist watch.
   c. pound on the door, trying to get back in.
   d. notice that the street lamp is now a gas lamp.

Recalling Facts

2. When Mrs. Landers asks which army Corrigan served in, he tells her it was the
   a. Continental Army.
   b. Army of the Confederacy.
   c. Republican Army.
   d. Army of the Republic.

Identifying Cause and Effect

3. Corrigan is taken to jail from Ford's Theatre because he
   a. is dressed strangely.
   b. has been accused of assassinating the President.
   c. is causing a disturbance with his shouting.
   d. tried to get into the theater without a ticket.

Understanding Main Ideas

4. Jonathan Wellington really takes custody of Corrigan because he
   a. wants to help a veteran.
   b. wants to stop him from warning people about the assassination attempt.
   c. wants to know more about time travel.
   d. believes Corrigan and wants to know more so he can stop the assassination.

Recognizing Literary
Elements (Setting)

5. This play takes place in the years
   a. 1865 and 1958.
   b. 1858 and 1958.
   c. 1858 and 1965.
   d. 1865 and 1965.

INTERPRETING   To complete these sentences, you may look back at the play if you'd like.

Making Inferences

6. When the Police Captain says of Corrigan, "Let him sleep it off," he is implying that Corrigan is
   a. drunk.
   b. from another time.
   c. tired.
   d. a dangerous criminal.

Analyzing

7. One Police Officer takes Corrigan's warnings seriously when other people do not because he
   a. is young.
   b. believes everything he hears, no matter how ridiculous.
   c. is open to new ideas.
   d. genuinely likes people.

Predicting Outcomes

8. If another club member were sent back in time to the day of Lincoln's assassination, he probably would
   a. find a way to stop the assassination.
   b. not even try to stop the assassination.
   c. not be able to stop the assassination either.
   d. assassinate the President.

Making
Generalizations

9. William's grandfather would give this advice to people who want successful careers:
   a. Listen to your bosses and do what they say.
   b. Save your money for a rainy day.
   c. Think for yourself and do what you think is right.
   d. Never follow orders.

Recognizing Literary Elements (Theme)

10. One of the messages of this play is that
     a. one should never doubt unproved theories.
     b. people who try hard can accomplish anything.
     c. time travel can be fun.
     d. some things were just meant to be.

Now check your answers with your teacher. Study the questions you answered incorrectly. What types of questions were they? Talk with your teacher about ways to work on those skills.

Plot

You probably have heard that literature is like life in many ways. The characters you meet in stories and plays can be similar to people you meet in real life. The problems fictional characters face are often similar to the ones real people face too.

However, in one way, literature is different from life. Life is messy. Every day, a series of seemingly unrelated events takes place in your life. One event doesn't always directly cause the next one. Events often seem independent and unconnected to each other. Literature, on the other hand, is neat and tidy. In plays and other literature, events are directly connected. An author includes only those events that move the plot along. Especially in a play, the author plans the plot so it can be communicated efficiently through the words and actions of the characters.

In a typical play a character is introduced, a problem is identified, and the problem gets more and more complicated. Finally the problem reaches a turning point and the story winds down to the end. Any details that don't fit this formula are left out.

In this unit, you will look at the ways in which author Rod Serling has developed his plot in order to tell the story in *Back There*:

1. Serling introduces the characters and the setting in the introduction, or exposition. Then, he presents the problem (conflict) that the main character must face.

2. Serling lets the tension and excitement build until the turning point, or climax.

3. He tells what happens to the characters after the climax, and then he ends the play.

LESSON 1 | EXPOSITION AND RISING ACTION

When you begin to read a play, you enter a new world. Sometimes you find yourself in a new time—the past or the future. You always find yourself in a new place—a different city, a forest, an unfamiliar backyard. It is the author's job to help you get used to the new world as quickly as possible. That is what the author does in the *exposition*, or introduction of the play. He or she describes the setting and introduces you to the characters who will be taking part in the action. In a play, the author usually uses stage directions to convey the introductory information, as Rod Serling does in the beginning of *Back There*:

> (*Near a large front entrance of double doors is a name plaque in brass which reads "The Washington Club, Founded 1858." In the main hall of the building is a large paneled foyer with rooms leading off on either side. An attendant,* **William**, *carrying a tray of drinks, crosses the hall and enters one of the rooms. There are four men sitting around in the aftermath of a card game.* **Peter Corrigan** *is the youngest, then two middle-aged men named* **Whitaker** *and* **Millard**, *and* **Jackson**, *the oldest, a white-haired man in his sixties, who motions the tray from the attendant over to the table.*)

Later, as the play's action begins, you learn more about the characters and about the exact time and place where events happen. As you enter the play's world, the men described in the opening stage directions are having a discussion. Go back and skim Scene 1. Notice that Corrigan has the most lines. What do you learn about Corrigan from his interaction with the other men in this scene?

From what he says to Whitaker, Millard, and Jackson, you can tell that Corrigan is the character who is most doubtful about the possibility of time travel. He is logical and doesn't seem to care about theories that cannot be proved. From his kindness to William, you also learn that he has compassion for others and acts upon what he feels is right.

The exposition does more than introduce the characters and setting. It also introduces the *conflict*, or problem, that the characters face. A conflict can be between two or more characters, or it can be between opposing forces. It is up to the characters to try and overcome the conflict.

In the next part of the plot, called the *rising action*, things happen that make the problem more complicated. One event leads to the next, and the tension builds. In *Back There*, the conflict begins when Corrigan leaves the Washington Club and discovers that he is no longer in the year 1965. Almost immediately, he knows that he is somewhere in the past. After he decides to find his home, events sweep him away. Read this part of the play to see how the Lieutenant and his wife add a new dimension to the conflict.

Corrigan.   *(takes a step down the stairs, staring at the* **Lieutenant***)* You're going to a play tonight? *(The* **Lieutenant** *nods.)*

Girl.   *(at the door)* We may or we may not, depending on when my husband makes up his mind to get a carriage in time to have dinner and get to the theatre.

Corrigan.   What theatre? *What* play?

Lieutenant.   Ford's Theatre, of course.

Corrigan.   *(looking off, his voice intense)* Ford's Theatre. Ford's Theatre.

Lieutenant.   Are you all right? I mean do you feel all right?

Corrigan.   *(whirls around to stare at him)* What's the name of the play?

Lieutenant.   *(exchanges a look with his wife)* I beg your pardon?

Corrigan. The play. The one you're going to tonight at Ford's Theatre. What's the name of it?

Girl. It's called "Our American Cousin."

Corrigan. (*again looks off thoughtfully*) "Our American Cousin" and Lincoln's going to be there.

Corrigan. (*looks from one to the other, first toward the* **Landlady** *on the steps, then down toward the* **Lieutenant** *and his wife*) And it's April 14th, 1865, isn't it? Isn't it April 14th, 1865? (*He starts down the steps without waiting for an answer. The* **Lieutenant** *stands in front of him.*)

Lieutenant. Really, sir, I'd call your actions most strange.

Suddenly Corrigan realizes that he has been taken back to the very day and place of Abraham Lincoln's assassination. A new problem has been introduced that further complicates the plot. How can Corrigan stop the assassination? From now on, his actions will become more and more urgent until the play reaches its climax.

EXERCISE 1

Read this passage and use what you have learned in this lesson to answer the questions that follow.

(*On one side is the stage door with a sign over it reading "Ford's Theatre."* **Corrigan** *turns the corridor into the alley at a dead run. He stops directly under the light, looks left and right, then vaults over the railing and pounds on the stage door.*)

Corrigan. (*shouting*) Hey! Hey, let me in! President Lincoln is going to be shot tonight! (*He continues to pound on the door and shout.*)

1. Corrigan reacts to the situation very quickly and forcefully. What qualities about him make you expect this reaction?

2. How do Corrigan's actions in this passage cause what happens next?

Now check your answers with your teacher. Review this part of the lesson if you don't understand why an answer was incorrect.

 WRITING ON YOUR OWN 1

Use what you have learned so far to plan the beginning of a short play about a trip. Follow these steps:

- Decide on a setting for your play, and describe it in a few sentences. Include details about both the time and the place.
- Think about the characters who will be in your play. What kinds of characters would you be likely to find in your chosen setting? Briefly describe two or three characters.
- Consider where and when the play is set and the characters you have chosen. What major conflict will your characters face? Make a list of possible conflicts. Then choose the one you find most interesting.
- Last, write a list of possible events in your play. They don't need to be stated in full sentences. Make sure there is a connection between events.

LESSON 2 — CLIMAX, OR TURNING POINT

The *climax*, or turning point, is the point of greatest tension in a story. In some ways, it is like the top of a mountain. Before mountain climbers reach the top, they must climb higher and higher and put themselves in greater danger with every step. When they reach the top of the mountain, they have finally reached their goal. Since they can't go any farther up, the only way to go is down.

Just like mountain climbers, when characters reach the climax of a story, they have reached the height of the action and can only go back down. The only thing left for the writer to do after the climax is to tie up loose ends and finish the story.

In *Back There*, Corrigan has been trying desperately to stop the assassination of President Lincoln. When the young police officer rescues him, Corrigan hopes he has one last chance. Note the desperation in his voice as you read the following passage. Find the point where the story turns—where it changes suddenly and cannot be reversed.

> **Corrigan.**　He said his name was Wellington! And *that's why he drugged me.* (*He grabs the* **Police Officer** *again.*) He gave me wine and he drugged me. He didn't want me to stop him. He's the one who's going to do it. Listen, you've got to get to that theatre. You've got to stop him. John Wilkes Booth! He's going to kill Lincoln. Look, get out of here now! Will you stop him? Will you— (*He stops abruptly, his eyes look up. All three people turn to look toward the window. There's the sound of crowd noises building, suggestive of excitement, and then almost a collective wail, a mournful, universal chant that comes from the streets, and as the sound builds we suddenly hear intelligible words that are part of the mob noise.*)
>
> **Voices.**　The President's been shot. President Lincoln's been assassinated. Lincoln is dying.

The news of Lincoln's assassination stops the rise in tension. After that climactic point, the action takes a downward turn and the play soon ends.

EXERCISE 2

Read the following passage in which the characters first learn of Lincoln's assassination. Use what you have learned in this lesson to answer the questions.

Voices. The President's been shot. President Lincoln's been assassinated. Lincoln is dying.

(The **Landlady** *suddenly bursts into tears. The* **Police Officer** *rises to his feet, his face white.*)

Police Officer. Oh my dear God! You were right. You *did* know. Oh . . . my . . . dear . . . God! (*He turns, almost trance-like, and walks out of the room. The* **Landlady** *follows him.* **Corrigan** *rises weakly and goes to the window, staring out at the night and listening to the sounds of a nation beginning its mourning. He closes his eyes and puts his head against the windowpane and with fruitless, weakened smashes, hits the side of the window frame as he talks.*)

Corrigan. I tried to tell you. I tried to warn you. Why didn't anybody listen? Why? Why didn't anyone listen to me? (*His fist beats a steady staccato on the window frame.*)

1. How do the attitudes of the Landlady and the Police Officer change after the climax of this play?

2. What are Corrigan's feelings before he hears the tragic news? What are his feelings after the climax?

Now check your answers with your teacher. Review this part of the lesson if you don't understand why an answer was incorrect.

WRITING ON YOUR OWN ⌷2⌷

Remember that you are planning a short play about a trip. First review what you wrote for Writing On Your Own 1. Then do the following:

- Decide how the conflict and rising action you described earlier will end. Will your characters succeed or fail in their attempts to solve the problem?
- Think about the climax of your story. It will be the point of highest tension or excitement. Since plays are built using words and actions, you must decide who will speak or act during the climax of your play. Make a list of characters who will be present during this scene.
- Now write the scene in which the climax of your play occurs. Show how this moment is the turning point of the story. Use the format that you find in this play to indicate who is talking and what actions are taking place.

LESSON 3 | FALLING ACTION AND RESOLUTION

The *falling action* describes all the events that happen after the climax. In some stories, the falling action is over very quickly. Not much needs to be ironed out or explained for the reader. In other stories, however, the falling action takes a bit longer. Readers need to know how the characters react to—or change as a result of—the events that came before.

During the falling action in *Back There*, two major events take place. They don't have the tension that the earlier part of the play had, but they are essential to the plot. First, Corrigan—who has been carried forward to the year 1965 again—excitedly reports his findings on time travel:

(**Corrigan** *walks past the attendant, through the big double doors that lead to the card room as in Act I. His three friends are in the middle of a discussion. The fourth man at the table, sitting in his seat, has his back to the camera.*)

Millard. (*looking up*) Hello, Pete. Come on over and join tonight's bull session. It has to do with the best ways of amassing a fortune. What are your tried-and-true methods?

Corrigan.   (*His voice is intense and shaky.*) We were talking about time travel, about going back in time.

Jackson.   (*dismissing it*) Oh that's old stuff. We're on a new tack now. Money and the best ways to acquire it.

Corrigan.   Listen . . . listen, I want to tell you something. This is true. If you go back into the past you can't change anything. (*He takes another step toward the table.*) Understand? You can't change anything.

Since the men's previous discussion is the reason that Corrigan was sent back in time, it is important that the author tie up this loose end. The club members need to know what Corrigan has learned.

The conclusion, or end, of a story is also known as its *resolution.* Authors don't simply stop writing when they can't think of anything else to say. Instead, they must make sure that all the unanswered questions have been answered and that the reader or audience knows that the story is over. At the resolution of *Back There*, a narrator's voice is heard:

Narrator's Voice.   Mr. Peter Corrigan, lately returned from a place "Back There"; a journey into time with highly questionable results. Proving, on one hand, that the threads of history are woven tightly and the skein of events cannot be undone; but, on the other hand, there are small fragments of tapestry that *can* be altered. Tonight's thesis, to be taken as you will, in *The Twilight Zone!*

As often happens in *The Twilight Zone* series, the play ends on an uncertain note. Corrigan's experiences have taught us a little about time and fate, but we can't say that we understand these subjects completely. Which past events can be altered and which can't? We will never know.

EXERCISE ⟨3⟩

Read this passage from the last scene, in which playwright Rod Serling throws in a new and unexpected twist during the falling action. Use what you have learned in this lesson to answer the questions that follow the passage.

Corrigan. William? (*He sees the attendant from Act I but now meticulously dressed, a middle-aged millionaire obviously, with a totally different manner, who puts a cigarette in a holder with manicured hands in the manner of a man totally accustomed to wealth.* **William** *looks up and smiles.*)

William. Oh yes. My method for achieving security is far the best. You simply inherit it. It comes to you in a beribboned box. I was telling the boys here, Corrigan. My great grandfather was on the police force here in Washington on the night of Lincoln's assassination. He went all over town trying to warn people that something might happen. (*He holds up his hands in a gesture.*) How he figured it out, nobody seems to know. It's certainly not recorded any place. But because there was so much publicity, people never forgot him. He became a police chief, then a councilman, did some wheeling and dealing in land and became a millionaire. What do you say we get back to our bridge, gentlemen? (**Jackson** *takes the cards and starts to shuffle.* **William** *turns in his seat once again.*)

William. How about it, Corrigan? Take a hand?

Corrigan. Thank you, William, no. I think I'll . . . I think I'll just go home. (*He turns very slowly and starts*

toward the exit. Over his walk we hear the whispered,
hushed murmurings of the men at the table.)

1. Corrigan has just stated that nothing can be changed in time. How does William's situation prove that statement false? How do you know that William's wealth is directly connected to Corrigan's trip to the past?

2. What is Corrigan's reaction to this new information about William's wealth? Why is that reaction believable at this stage in the play?

   Now check your answers with your teacher. Review this part of the lesson if you don't understand why an answer was incorrect.

 WRITING ON YOUR OWN 3

In this exercise you will plan the falling action and resolution of your play. Follow these steps:

- Review your assignments for the other writing exercises in this unit. You've already decided what will happen in the rising action and the climax. Now decide how the characters will react to the events that have taken place. Make a list of about three to five events that will happen after the climax.
- What will be the final words of the play? Who will be present in the last scene? What will the audience see last? Write a paragraph describing the words, actions, and setting of the end of the play.

DISCUSSION GUIDES

1. Corrigan gets a chance to travel in time to a crucial day in American history. If you could travel back to a particular day in American history, what date would it be? Work with a group to list particular days you would like to visit and explain why you would like to visit them. Explain what you would want to do there and whom you would like to meet. Is there an outcome that you would like to influence in some way? Why or why not?

2. Mr. Wellington turns out to be John Wilkes Booth in disguise. How much do you know about Booth—the events that led him to assassinate President Lincoln and what happened to him after that night? With a partner, research John Wilkes Booth's life. Then use your research to present two interviews to the rest of the class. In the first interview, one of you should be the interviewer and the other should portray Booth. In the second interview, the person being interviewed should be his brother, Edwin Booth.

3. Time travel is a favorite theme in many science-fiction stories. Work with a small group to list as many stories, novels, movies, television shows, and plays as you can that deal with time travel. Then compare and contrast the stories in the following ways. Have one member of the group record the group's responses.

   - how the characters were transported through time
   - where they went—both place and time
   - the problems they faced
   - how they solved their problems
   - whether they were able to return to the original time
   - how the story ended

CREATE A STORYBOARD

In this unit you have seen how authors develop the plots of their plays. Now you will create a storyboard that will show the plot of your original play about a trip. Follow these steps to complete your storyboard.

If you have questions about the writing process, refer to Using the Writing Process (page 261).

- Review the writing assignments you completed in this unit. They should include the following: 1) your description of a setting and characters and your list of story events, 2) the climactic scene from your play, 3) a list of events in the falling action and a paragraph describing the last scene.
- Use sheets of construction paper to make a storyboard. First use your notes from previous exercises to draw the most important scenes. Draw only one scene on each sheet of paper. Then at the bottom of each page, copy one of the sentences from the notecards you created earlier. Make sure each sentence describes what is going on in the picture above it.
- If you don't feel confident about your drawing ability, you may want to work with a partner who can draw the scenes for you. Otherwise, you may wish to make a simple diagram of each scene, identifying the characters and showing where they would be standing.
- As you work on your storyboard, you may discover that you need more scenes to tell the story, or you may change your mind about some scenes. Make any necessary changes.
- Proofread your scene descriptions for spelling, grammar, punctuation, and capitalization errors.
- Arrange your pages in order on a large poster so that all the scenes and their descriptions can be seen at once. If possible, arrange them on the chalkboard or a bulletin board so others can see and read your plot.
- When you take your pages down, store them in your writing portfolio.

Characters

When the Rattlesnake Sounds

by Alice Childress

INTRODUCTION

ABOUT THE SELECTION

Among the conductors on the Underground Railroad, none was more famous than Harriet Tubman (1821?–1913). Born a slave, this remarkable woman escaped to the North in 1849, yet she returned to the South at least 19 times to lead more than 300 slaves to freedom. She was supported by such anti-slavery groups as the Society of Friends, or Quakers. When the Civil War began, Tubman served as a guide for Northern forces. After the war, she worked for the civil rights of African Americans and women.

When the Rattlesnake Sounds is based on an actual event. To raise funds for her next trip South, Tubman worked for a summer as a laundress in a New Jersey hotel. The fictional conversation presented in this play draws on Tubman's own thoughts and words, as reported by friends and those who heard her speeches.

"Captain Brown" was John Brown (1800–1859), the white anti-slavery leader who, in 1859, tried to incite a slave rebellion. His small abolitionist force took the U.S. arsenal at Harper's Ferry, Virginia (now West Virginia), but was captured the next day. Brown was convicted of treason and hanged.

ABOUT THE AUTHOR

Alice Childress (1920–) is a writer of plays, novels, and nonfiction. Born in Charleston, South Carolina, she grew up and was educated in Harlem, in New York City. She was a member of the American Negro Theater for 10 years but left acting to write plays. She was the first African-American woman to have a play professionally produced on the American stage (1952), and the first woman to win an Obie Award for best off-Broadway production for her play *Trouble in Mind* (1955).

Although Childress never finished high school, she served in the late 1960s as resident playwright and scholar at Harvard University's Radcliffe Institute for Independent Study. Her first novel for young readers was *A Hero Ain't Nothin But a Sandwich* (1973), which was nominated for both a Newbery Medal and a National Book Award.

ABOUT THE LESSONS

The lessons that follow *When the Rattlesnake Sounds* focus on how an author develops the characters in a play. Although Childress shows three characters in one setting, having a single conversation, you will come to appreciate each character as a separate individual with a distinct personality. You will be able to imagine each character in other situations and know how she would react to other problems. These lessons will help you understand what playwrights do to make their characters seem so real.

 WRITING: DEVELOPING A CHARACTER

In most cases, an author has some idea of what his or her characters will be like long before beginning to write a play. In some cases, as with Harriet Tubman in *When the Rattlesnake Sounds*, the character is an actual person from history. In other cases, as with Celia in this play, the author creates a fictional character who can face up to the play's conflict, or problem, in a special way.

During this unit, you will investigate ways to create and develop a character. You will use your skills to present your character in a short scene. This activity will start you thinking about what makes a character memorable:

- Think of three or more famous people you would like to meet and list their names.
- For each person on your list, make a cluster map like the one below. Write the name of the person in the center circle. Write words or phrases in the linked circles that describe that person's most important qualities and achievements. Then include details about the qualities that make or made this person famous and interesting.

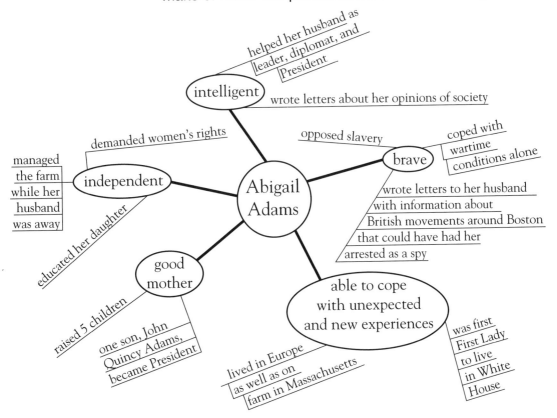

AS YOU
READ

These questions will help you look at how playwright Alice Childress developed the characters in *When the Rattlesnake Sounds*. Keep the questions in mind as you read the play.

- What do you learn about each character from the playwright's description of her?
- What do you learn about each character from what the other characters say about her?
- What do you learn about each character from what she does or is reported to do?
- What does each character say about her own thoughts and feelings? Do any of the characters' beliefs or attitudes change from the beginning of the play to the end?

When the Rattlesnake Sounds

by Alice Childress

SETTING

Time: *Very close to the end of legal slavery*

Place: *Cape May, New Jersey*

Scene: *A hotel laundry room*

CHARACTERS

Harriet Tubman

An experienced leader who knows how to handle people with firmness . . . and love. Actually she was a little woman, five feet tall, but for the purposes of a play the qualities of leadership and compassion are more important than actual appearance. She is in her early forties.

Lennie

A strong, determined, no-nonsense kind of young woman. She is used to hard work and is perhaps physically stronger than Harriet, but does not have the tact to handle leadership. She is about twenty-five years old.

Celia

A very attractive young woman who has certainly been more sheltered than the other two. Celia is also a dedicated person . . . but she sees the freedom struggle in romantic terms . . . and has the tendency to get fed up when the going is grubby and ordinary.

There is a pile of loose laundry on the floor waiting to be done . . . much with flounces and lace to suggest the summer clothing of ladies in the 1860's. There are three washtubs filled with water and laundry; in each tub is a washboard. **Harriet**, **Lennie**, *and* **Celia** *are washing clothes. The women are dressed in calico dresses and aprons.* **Harriet** *and* **Lennie** *work vigorously, absorbed in the task.* **Celia** *is slowing up and finally stops.*

Celia. *(cautiously watching* **Harriet** *and* **Lennie***)* Lord, I'm tired. *(others keep working)* Seem like we workin way past our dinnertime, don't it? Harriet? Lennie?

Lennie. Not much past dinner. It feels like about one o'clock.

Harriet. We're gonna stop an eat by 'n by. We'll put out five bundles of wash today. Yesterday was only four.

Celia. *Only* four? When I went to bed last night, I cried, I was so bone-weary. Only? How can four bundles of wash be *only*?

Harriet. Just a while longer, Celia. Let's sing. When you singin, the work goes fast. You pick a song, Lennie.

Lennie. *(decides to pick one that will annoy* **Celia***)* Wadin in the water, wadin in the water (children). Wadin in the water, God gonna trouble the water. *(**Harriet** joins her in singing.)*

Celia. *(drying her hands on her apron)* I want my dinner now. I'm hungry.

Lennie. We all hungry, Celia. Can't you hold out a little more?

Celia. If we *all* hungry, why don't we *all* eat? We been up since seven this mornin . . . workin. For what? Why?

Lennie. You know why! We got to finish five bundles.

Celia. *(to the heavens above)* Five bundles for what?

Lennie. For a dollar and a quarter, that's what! *(grumbling)* I'm tellin you . . . some people.

Harriet. *(Sensing trouble, she stops washing.)* Celia is right, Lennie. It's not good to kill yourself workin.

Lennie. *(in anger)* She knows why we're doin it, Harriet. Some people . . . I'm tellin you.

Harriet. *(firmly)* Let's have our dinner, Lennie.

Lennie. *(her eyes on **Celia**)* Did you fix it again, Harriet? We suppose to take turns. I take a turn, you take a turn, then . . . .

Harriet. *(hastily cutting her off)* I got some nice corn bread and some side meat. The coffee should be ready. *(handing out paper parcels to the girls)* We need to rest awhile. Here, Celia, and that's yours, Lennie. *(going back to her tub)* I'll just wash out these few more pieces before my water turns cold.

Lennie. I ain't restin unless you rest too. Not like some people I know.

Celia. She keep sayin *some people*. Wonder who she means?

Harriet. *(with a sigh)* I'll stop too.

Celia. *(looking at the pile of unwashed clothes as she unwraps her lunch)* White folks love white clothes and they love to sit in the grass too . . . and I'm sick of scrubbin grass stains.

Harriet. Well, we need the money.

Celia. *(puts down her lunch and snatches up a flouncy white dress)* Look at all the money *they* got. This cost every bit of twelve dollars. *(imitating the hotel guests)* Spendin the summer in a big hotel, ridin round in carriages. *(drops her airy act and goes back to anger)* If just one of em give us what she spend in a week . . . we wouldn't have to work two months in no hotel laundry.

Lennie.   I got a life-size picture of them givin you that much money. They ain't gonna give you nothin, so you better be glad you got the chance to *earn* some.

Celia.   Scrubbin! Ain't that a damn somethin to be glad about? Excuse me, Harriet, I meant to say dern or drat.

Harriet.   Celia got somethin on her mind, and she need to talk, so let her talk, Lennie. But no dammin, dernin, or drattin either. All here got more manners than to cuss.

Lennie.   *(as she looks at **Harriet**'s food)* Is that your dinner? You ain't got no meat on your bread, Harriet.

Harriet.   I don't too much like meat.

Lennie.   I know who do. Some people.

Celia.   *(bursting out at **Harriet**)* Stop sayin that! You do too like meat! Stop makin out like you don't. You goin without so you can save another nickel. Yall drivin me outta my head. Maybe I'm just not suited for this kinda thing.

Lennie.   But I am, huh?

Harriet.   *(quietly and seriously)* You tired of this bargain we made? You sorry about it and don't know how to quit?

Lennie.   *(flaring with anger)* She promised and she got to stick by it! Your father is a *deacon of the church* . . . and if you don't keep your word, you gonna bring disgrace down on him and *every member* of your family.

Harriet.   Lennie, don't be so brash. Mother and father is one thing . . . child is another. Each one stands upon his own deeds. She don't have to stay. Celia, you can go if you want.

Celia.   I don't really want to get out of it. But I want *some* of my money for myself. I'm tired of sleepin three in a room. I want to spend a little of the money . . . just a little, Harriet. Buy a few treats.

Lennie.   She's jealous of them rich white ladies . . . cause they got silk parasols to match they dresses. I heard her say it. "Wish I had me a silk parasol."

Harriet.   We eatin and sleepin. We spend for that and nothin more . . . that was the bargain.

Celia.   (*to* **Lennie**) I could own a silk parasol *and* carry it . . . without actin like a field hand.

Harriet.   I been a field hand, children. Harness to a plow like a workhorse.

Celia.   Scuse me, I'm sorry.

Lennie.   (*really sarcastic*) Celia, that don't sound nothin like them big speeches you used to make in church meetin. (*mocking* **Celia**) "I'll die for my freedom!" . . . Had everybody whoopin and hollerin every time you open your mouth, whole church stompin and shoutin amen.

Celia.   (*sadly*) I remember how it was.

(*The women remove their aprons and Harriet takes her place center stage. Church music in from off-stage or recording of "The Old Ship of Zion," or any of the A. M. E. Zion songs. Harriet Tubman was a member of that church. She addresses the audience as though they are the congregation.*)

Harriet.   (*Music and humming are in low as she speaks.*) God bless you, brothers and sisters, bless you, children.

Offstage Voices plus Lennie and Celia.   Amen . . . Amen . . . Bless God.

Harriet.   I thank the good Lord for the support of the African Methodist Episcopal Zion Church in the freedom struggle. There is comfort and good fellowship here.

Church Voices.   Yes, Lord. Amen.

Harriet.   Not like hidin in the bitter cold, with the huntin dogs followin you down with no restin place in sight.

We had to give the little babies paregoric[1] so they wouldn't cry and let the paddy-rollers know where to find us. We crossed some lonely roads and rivers . . . the dark of the night around us, the clouds cuttin off the sight of the North Star. But everything was all right cause where I go . . . God goes . . . and I carry a gun . . . two guns . . . a hand pistol and a shoulder rifle . . . just in case the Lord tell me I got to use it!

Church Voices.   Amen! Speak! Praise the holy name! Amen!

Harriet.   I thank the Father for the help and assistance of the Society of Friends and the abolitionists,[2] and all well-wishers.

Church Voices.   Amen, Amen, Amen.

Harriet.   But as I put my hand to the plow to do the work of Freedom, so I also put *my money* into the work. I have none now, so I will spend my summer washin and ironin so that when the fall come I have *some of my own* to put . . . to buy food, medicine, paregoric for the babies, and ammunition for the pistol. . . . Lord grant I never use it. Any ladies here want to go with me to wash clothes and give the money to free our slave brethren?

Lennie.   (*stands by Harriet's side*) If you would have me, Mrs. Tubman, it would be the greatest honor, a great honor indeed.

Harriet.   Thank you, my daughter.

Celia.   (*stands up and throws her arms out in a Joan of Arc gesture*) I'll die for my freedom! Take me, Sister! I'm ready to fight the good fight. Hallelujah!

Church Voices.   (**Celia** *has set the church to rocking.*) Glory! Glory! Hallelujah! Fight the good fight! Amen! (*Music fades out as women don their aprons again.*)

---

[1] medicine that causes drowsiness in most people

[2] person who favors abolishing, or getting rid of, a particular law or custom; specifically one who favored abolishing slavery

Celia. I remember how it was, Lennie, and the promise I made. But how much can we get like this? Maybe if *everybody* worked and gave their money to the Underground, it would mean somethin. This way I just can't see it, but I believe in freedom and I understand.

Harriet. Ain't no such thing as only "understandin." Understandin mean action. You have to look after what *Celia* does . . . and if *nobody else* do nothin, you got to. Freedom is just a baby, and you its mother. You don't stop lovin and carin for it just cause others don't care.

Celia. Maybe it's easy to talk like that when you Moses. It's easy to kill yourself for somethin when thousands of people be cheerin you on. Lennie and Celia don't mean nothin to nobody. We could die here and nobody would know or care.

Lennie. Don't you talk for me! Ain't nothin greater to me than to be able to say . . . "I, Lennie Brown, scrubbed clothes side by side with Moses." If you lookin for praise, you don't belong here.

Harriet. Children, let us keep peace. We act like we hate each other worse than we hate the slaveowner.

Celia. I know what I sound like. . . . *(falls at* **Harriet**'s *feet and holds out her hands)* Oh, Harriet, my hands are skinned sore.

Lennie. Do, Jesus, look at Celia's hands.

Harriet. *(turns Celia's head and searches for the truth)* But it ain't your hands that's really botherin you. It ain't food, it ain't sleepin three in a room, and it ain't about silk parasols. What's botherin you, Celia?

Celia. I'm so shame for feelin the way I do. Lord knows I'm shame.

Harriet. Tell it. Speak your shame.

Celia.   I'm *scared*. If these people in this hotel knew who you was. Forty thousand dollars' reward out for you!

Lennie.   (*dashes to the door to see if anyone is around to listen*) Hush your fool mouth! Moses got the charm. Slave holder will never catch Moses.

Celia.   I'm so shame. All those other things just lies. I ain't so terrible tired. I'm just scared and shame cause I'm afraid. Me talkin so big. Sure, I'd work all summer and give the money to the Underground. It did sound so good in the meetin where it was all warm and friendly. Now I'm scared of gettin into trouble. I never been no slave. And I'm scared of nothin round me but white folks.

Lennie.   We ain't got no room for no rabbity, timid kinda women in this work.

Harriet.   Oh, yes, Lennie, we got room for the timid and the brave. Poor little Celia. Child, you lookin at a woman who's been plenty afraid. When the rattlesnake sounds a warnin . . . it's time to be scared. Ain't that natural? When I run away was nobody to cheer me on . . . don't you think I was scared?

Lennie.   But you got to freedom.

Harriet.   (*The feeling of a "meeting" begins.*) Oh, but when I found I'd crossed that line! There was such a glory over everything. The sun came shinin like gold through the trees.

Lennie.   (*feels she is at church meeting*) You felt like you was in heaven! You was free!

Harriet.   But there was no one to welcome me in the land of freedom. I was a stranger in a strange land. My home, after all, was down in the old cabin quarters with the ones I knew and loved . . . my slave mother and father, brothers, sisters and friends. Aunt Day . . . she used to be midwife, tend the sick, bury the dead. Two field hands I knew, they used to ease some the work off the women who was expectin. There I was standin on free land, with my heart back down there with them. What good is freedom without your people?

Lennie.   Go on, Harriet!

Harriet.   And so to this solemn resolution I come: As I was free . . . *they* would be free also.

Lennie.   Praise God, that's Harriet Tubman!

Harriet.   Sometimes I was scared in the icy river. Chilled to the bone and just might drown.

Lennie.   But you got cross.

Harriet.   I was scared in the dark and the swamp . . . but I come to the light. Most times I was full of hatred for the white folks.

Lennie.   And you came to the Friends.

Harriet.   And I came to John Brown. (*offstage music . . . soft violin . . . sound of voices ad-libbing at a reception*) There was this big, fine affair. A reception. Abolitionist reception. The ladies were all dressed in lovely gowns, made by free labor. I was in my best too . . . but that wasn't too much better than what I'm standin in. They had pretty cakes and a punch bowl . . . the grandest party. Violin music . . . what you call elegant. There was a goodly crowd, and I was way on the other side of the room, away from the main door where the people would enter. Everybody called him Captain Brown . . . Captain. (**Harriet** *moves to the far side of the stage and turns toward the opposite door to illustrate the distance between her and Captain Brown.*)

Harriet.   The whisper started way down the hall and came through the room . . . "It's Captain Brown. He's here. Captain Brown is about to enter." Then he came in the door. He was a fine, stern-lookin gentleman . . . goodness glowed from his face like a burnin light. The room got quiet. He looked all around until he saw me. Mind now, we had never met. The ladies and gentlemen were all tryin to meet him. . . . Oh, it was Captain, Captain, Captain. He held up his hand. There was silence, then he said . . . "The first I see is General Tubman. The second is General Tubman. The third is General Tubman." He crossed the room and bowed to me . . . and I shook his hand.

Lennie.   And he died for us, didn't he?

Harriet.   Celia, he was a brave man, but I believe he must have been scared sometimes. But he did what he had to do.

Celia.   I guess he was just brave. Some folks braver than others.

Harriet.   I was with hundreds of brave black men on battle-ground. I was there, Celia. We saw the lightning and that was the guns, then we heard the thunder and that was the big guns, then we heard the rain falling. . . . And that was the drops of blood. And when we came to get the crops, it was dead men we reaped.

Lennie.   Fightin for us to be free. I guess they musta been scared sometimes.

Harriet.   Give me your hand, Celia. Look, see the skin broken across the knuckles. Counta you some man or woman gonna have warm socks and boots to help em get to freedom. See the cuts the lye soap put in your skin. Counta you some little baby is gonna be born on free soil. It won't matter to him that you was afraid, won't matter that he did not know your name. Won't nothin count ceptin he's free. A livin monument to Celia's work. (**Celia** cries.) You go to the room and rest. Maybe you might want to stay here after you think about it.

Lennie.   Sure, Celia . . . think bout it. We can manage. And if you want to go home, we won't hold it against you. I ought not to have said what I did. Sometimes I get scared myself . . . but it makes me act evil *and* brave, you know?

Celia.   I don't want to go home. Guess there's worse things than fear. I'm glad to know I don't have to be shame about it.

Harriet.   That's right. If you was home doin nothin, what would you have to be fraid bout? That's when a woman oughta feel shame, shame to her very soul.

Celia.   (*Gathers up clothes, places them in tub, starts working.* **Harriet** *goes to her tub.*) If we sing, the work goes faster.

Lennie.   (*goes to her tub*) Your time to pick a song, Celia.

Celia.   (**Celia** *starts scrubbing. They all work for a few moments. Celia has decided on a song. She sings out.*)

Oh, Lord, I don't feel no ways tired

Children, Oh, Glory Hallelujah

For I hope to shout *Glory* when this world is all on fire

Oh, Glory, Hallelujah

(*The others join her on the second round.*)

Oh, Lord, I don't feel no ways tired. . . .

CURTAIN

REVIEWING AND INTERPRETING

Record your answers to these questions in your personal literature notebook. Follow the directions for each part.

REVIEWING   Try to complete each of these sentences without looking back at the play.

Identifying Cause and Effect

1. Celia is washing clothes at a hotel because
   a. Harriet asked for help and Celia volunteered.
   b. this is her usual way of earning money.
   c. she is a slave and her owners gave her this job.
   d. she is tired and hungry.

Recalling Facts

2. Lennie criticizes Celia for
   a. doing a poor job at her washing.
   b. not giving Harriet more respect.
   c. complaining about being hungry and tired.
   d. using the word *damn*.

Understanding Main Ideas

3. The first time John Brown and Harriet Tubman were in the same room, Brown said, "The first I see is General Tubman. The second is General Tubman. The third is General Tubman." He meant that Harriet Tubman
   a. was a very large woman.
   b. was the most important person in the room.
   c. moved around so much that he saw her wherever he looked.
   d. set the fashion, and everyone else was trying to look like her.

Identifying Sequence

4. Of the four events listed below, this one actually occurs first:
   a. Celia and Lennie hear Harriet speak at church.
   b. Harriet meets John Brown.
   c. Celia admits to Harriet that she is frightened.
   d. Lennie criticizes Celia for stopping to eat lunch.

Recognizing Literary Elements (Setting)

5. The action of this play takes place
   a. in a laundry room.
   b. at a party attended by Harriet Tubman and John Brown.
   c. in a church where Harriet speaks.
   d. in a laundry room and a church.

INTERPRETING To complete these sentences, you may look back at the play if you'd like.

Analyzing

6. Harriet believes that holding a belief is not enough, and that everyone must take action to support beliefs. This is shown in her statement that
   a. "When you singin, the work goes fast."
   b. "When the rattlesnake sounds a warnin . . . it's time to be scared."
   c. "Mother and father is one thing . . . child is another. Each one stands upon his own deeds."
   d. "Freedom is just a baby, and you its mother. You don't stop lovin and carin for it just cause others don't care."

Making Inferences

7. After Celia complains about numerous things, Harriet tells her that "it ain't your hands that's really botherin you. It ain't food, it ain't sleeping three in a room, and it ain't about silk parasols." The following is probably *not* a reason for Harriet's statement:
   a. In her travels, Harriet has seen other frightened people, and she now recognizes fear in Celia.
   b. Harriet has heard that Celia has a bad reputation.
   c. Celia complains about too many things, as if she's looking for any believable reason to leave the work.
   d. Harriet is a caring person who senses the difference between outward irritation and deeper concerns.

Predicting Outcomes   **8.** In the weeks following this conversation, it is very likely that
a. Celia will join Harriet on a trip into slave territory.
b. Lennie and Celia will become best friends.
c. Celia will lose heart and give up working with Harriet and Lennie, despite her promise.
d. Celia will fulfill the promise she made to do laundry all summer.

Making   **9.** The most important idea that a modern audience should
Generalizations   get from this play is that
a. there were many causes of the Civil War.
b. we should not let fear keep us from doing what we believe is right.
c. Harriet Tubman considered John Brown a great man.
d. some people get along better with their coworkers than others.

Understanding the   **10.** In the church scene, the playwright calls for Offstage
Elements of a Play   Voices, but only the three women—Harriet, Lennie, and
(Staging)   Celia—appear on stage. The other people at the church are not brought on stage because
a. it would be too costly to get costumes for all the church members.
b. it keeps the focus on the problems raised in their discussion.
c. the stage would be too crowded with so many people on it.
d. the author didn't want to write for such a large cast of characters.

Now check your answers with your teacher. Study the questions you answered incorrectly. What types of questions were they? Talk with your teacher about ways to work on those skills.

Characters

Every play has characters, but some characters are more believable and memorable than others. Occasionally the actor who plays a role gives it a special quality. In such a case, the actor can bring more attention to a minor character than the play's main characters get. More often, however, the qualities that make a character memorable are given to him or her by the playwright. Even when you only read a play, you find it easy to imagine someone saying the lines and making the moves described in the stage directions. Afterward, you remember the character's words and actions as clearly as if you had heard and seen them.

It's not easy for a playwright to make every character seem like a complete person. That's why he or she usually concentrates on just a few important, or main, characters. The playwright may use the same techniques on less important, or minor, characters, but since they have fewer lines and actions, they usually are less memorable.

When the Rattlesnake Sounds has only three characters, but they are all main characters. In these lessons, you will look at what playwright Alice Childress includes in the play to help you learn about these three main characters:

1. Childress includes stage directions that describe each character's appearance and personality.

2. She includes comments in each character's dialogue that reveal things about the characters themselves and about the other characters.

3. She includes descriptions of each character's actions.

4. She includes descriptions of each character's thoughts, attitudes, and feelings.

LESSON 1   HOW CHARACTERS ARE DESCRIBED

When a play is being prepared for performance, the playwright is usually not around to help the actors develop the characters. There are ways, however, in which the playwright can tell the actors how their characters should appear to the audience. The playwright can describe each character in the introductory notes and stage directions, and he or she can include descriptions of each character in the dialogue of the other characters.

If you are reading a play rather than seeing a performance of it, you can learn about each character by reading the descriptions provided in the stage directions and in the other characters' dialogue. Alice Childress provides clear, direct descriptions of her three characters in the introductory notes of *When the Rattlesnake Sounds*. Read, for example, her description of Lennie:

> *A strong, determined, no-nonsense kind of young woman. She is used to hard work and is perhaps physically stronger than Harriet, but does not have the tact to handle leadership. She is about twenty-five years old.*

Although viewing audiences will not read this introductory paragraph about Lennie, the information in it will be visible on stage, in the way the actress looks and presents the character. And since readers will not see Lennie on stage, the introductory paragraph will help them visualize her as a practical, healthy, twenty-five-year-old woman. It will alert them to watch for further signs of her character as they read the play.

Even more important than the playwright's stage directions is what the characters say about each other in their dialogue. Notice, for example, how Lennie's descriptions of Celia bring out vividly Celia's love of showy, attention-getting gestures:

She's jealous of them rich white ladies . . . cause they got silk parasols to match they dresses. I heard her say it. "Wish I had me a silk parasol."

Celia, that don't sound nothin like them big speeches you used to make in church meetin. "I'll die for my freedom!" . . . Had everybody whoopin and hollerin every time you open your mouth, whole church stompin and shoutin amen.

Lennie's statements let us know about a side of Celia that she would not want Harriet to see.

EXERCISE 1

Read these excerpts. The first is the playwright's introductory paragraph about Harriet Tubman. The second comes from the dialogue as Lennie and Celia talk to Harriet. Use what you have learned in this lesson to answer the questions that follow the excerpts.

An experienced leader who knows how to handle people with firmness . . . and love. Actually she was a little woman, five feet tall, but for the purposes of a play the qualities of leadership and compassion are more important than actual appearance. She is in her early forties.

Lennie. *(as she looks at* **Harriet**'s *food)* Is that your dinner? You ain't got no meat on your bread, Harriet.

Harriet. I don't too much like meat.

Lennie. I know who do. Some people.

Celia. *(bursting out at* **Harriet**) Stop sayin that! You do too like meat! Stop makin out like you don't. You goin without so you can save another nickel. . . .

1. What two details do readers learn about Harriet's physical characteristics from the introductory paragraph? Will audience members necessarily learn about these details? Why or why not? Are these details important? Explain your answer.

2. In the scene in which Celia's lines appear, Harriet has explained that she has a meatless meal because she doesn't much like meat. What reason does Celia give for Harriet's choice? What can we learn about Harriet from the fact that she tries to hide the real reason for her actions?

3. How does the dialogue quoted here illustrate the description of Harriet Tubman in the introductory note?

Now check your answers with your teacher. Review this part of the lesson if you don't understand why an answer was incorrect.

 WRITING ON YOUR OWN 1

In this exercise you will use what you have learned in the lesson to introduce a character. Your character will be based closely on a real person. Follow these steps:

- Think of a problem you learned about in the news. It could involve injury or illness, loss of a job, or money difficulties. It could involve someone harming others by bullying them, tricking them, or stealing from them. Write several sentences describing the problem.
- Focus on one of the people involved in the problem. Did this person cause the problem, survive it, or solve it? Add several sentences to your description of the problem to tell about this person's role in it.
- Imagine you will write a scene about this matter. The main character in the scene will be based on the real person you just described. Give the character a made-up name.

Then decide which qualities of the real person (if any) you will give the made-up character. Decide, also, which new qualities you will give the character. Make a list of all the qualities, or if you'd like, write them on a cluster map like the ones you created earlier in the unit.

• Write an introductory note that would help a director choose an actor to play this character. When you are finished, put your writing in your portfolio. You will use it again in the lessons that follow.

LESSON 2

HOW CHARACTERS ACT

In forming an opinion about people, you probably consider everything about them—especially their actions. You probably look at how they talk and move, as well as what they say and do. In presenting complete characters, therefore, playwrights include dialogue and stage directions that give us this information.

Notice, for example, how the characters speak in *When the Rattlesnake Sounds*. Instead of standard English, they use a dialect that reflects their African heritage. A few of their words—such as *parasols* and *paregoric*—sound old-fashioned, but their conversational style sounds natural so we can easily picture them saying these words.

Dialogue and stage directions help readers understand what a character is doing and how he or she is doing it. Sometimes, however, stage directions can also indicate when the character is doing something that doesn't seem to match his or her words. Read this passage to see how the dialogue and the stage directions both help to clarify Lennie's behavior.

Celia.   If we *all* hungry, why don't we *all* eat? We been up since seven this mornin . . . workin. For what? Why?

Lennie.   You know why! We got to finish five bundles.

Celia.   *(to the heavens above)* Five bundles for what?

Lennie.   For a dollar and a quarter, that's what! *(grumbling)* I'm tellin you . . . some people.

Harriet.   *(Sensing trouble, she stops washing.)* Celia is right, Lennie. It's not good to kill yourself workin.

Lennie.   *(in anger)* She knows why we're doin it, Harriet. Some people . . . I'm tellin you.

Harriet.   *(firmly)* Let's have our dinner, Lennie.

Lennie.   *(her eyes on* **Celia***)* Did you fix it again, Harriet? We suppose to take turns. I take a turn, you take a turn, then . . . .

Harriet.   *(hastily cutting her off)* I got some nice corn bread and some side meat. The coffee should be ready. *(handing out paper parcels to the girls)* We need to rest awhile. Here, Celia, and that's yours, Lennie. *(going back to her tub)* I'll just wash out these few more pieces before my water turns cold.

Lennie.   I ain't restin unless you rest too. Not like some people I know.

Celia.   She keep sayin *some people*. Wonder who she means?

When Celia begins to complain, it is understandable that Lennie would show some irritation in exclaiming, "You know why!" But then she starts criticizing Celia with the phrase "some people," using it over and over just to irritate Celia. She twice rejects Harriet's efforts to keep the peace. Stage directions state that she keeps her eyes on Celia even when she speaks to Harriet. Lennie's words and actions in this passage characterize her as self-righteous and unsympathetic. It is her sarcastic comment that soon provokes Celia to attack Harriet:

Harriet. I don't too much like meat.

Lennie. I know who do. Some people.

Celia. (*bursting out at* **Harriet**) Stop sayin that! . . . .

EXERCISE 2

Reread the passage beginning on page 105 for information about Harriet. Then use what you have learned to answer the following questions.

1. To whom does Harriet direct her comments? Why do you suppose she chooses to deal with this person first?

2. Identify two words or phrases in the stage directions that tell about Harriet's manner of speaking. What actions does she take to try to avoid an argument?

3. What does Harriet do that shows her true feelings about quitting work for a lunch break?

Now check your answers with your teacher. Review this part of the lesson if you don't understand why an answer was incorrect.

WRITING ON YOUR OWN 2

In this exercise you will write a description of a character's actions that reveal something about him or her. Follow these steps:

- Choose a strong emotion, such as anger, fear, pride, love, or embarrassment. How could you present that emotion in pantomime? If you need some ideas, think about mimes you have seen. Recall some of the actions and expressions they used to indicate their emotions without speaking.

- Now think of a situation in which a character would express your chosen emotion. For example, a shopper in a store might be angry while returning a purchase or delighted to find just what he or she was searching for. A student embarrassed about not knowing an answer might be trying to avoid the attention of a teacher. Write a few sentences describing the character, the emotion, and the situation you will develop.
- Using the information from the above item, write a short scene with very little dialogue but plenty of stage directions to present the situation. Remember to indicate not only what the character does and says but also how he or she acts and talks.

LESSON 3   WHAT CHARACTERS SAY ABOUT THEMSELVES

So far you have learned about characters through descriptions of them, as well as through their actions and reactions. You also have learned about them through other characters' reactions to them. Frequently, characters make our task easier by stating directly what they think or feel. Read, for example, what Harriet says about how she felt when she escaped from her owner:

> . . . Child, you lookin at a woman who's been plenty afraid. When the rattlesnake sounds a warnin . . . it's time to be scared. Ain't that natural? When I run away was nobody to cheer me on . . . don't you think I was scared?

Harriet also directly states her reasons for going back into dangerous territory:

> But there was no one to welcome me in the land of freedom. I was a stranger in a strange land. My home, after all, was down in the old cabin quarters with the ones I

knew and loved . . . my slave mother and father, brothers, sisters and friends. Aunt Day . . . she used to be midwife, tend the sick, bury the dead. Two field hands I knew, they used to ease some the work off the women who was expectin. There I was standin on free land, with my heart back down there with them. What good is freedom without your people? . . . And so to this solemn resolution I come: As I was free . . . they *would be free also.*

EXERCISE 3

Read the following passage, which begins with Harriet speaking to Celia about her possible contribution to the abolitionist cause. Then use what you have learned in this lesson to answer the questions that follow the passage.

Harriet.   . . . Counta you some little baby is gonna be born on free soil. It won't matter to him that you was afraid, won't matter that he did not know your name. Won't nothin count ceptin he's free. A livin monument to Celia's work. (**Celia** *cries.*) You go to the room and rest. Maybe you might want to stay here after you think about it.

Lennie.   Sure, Celia . . . think bout it. We can manage. And if you want to go home, we won't hold it against you. I ought not to have said what I did. Sometimes I get scared myself . . . but it makes me act evil *and* brave, you know?

Celia.   I don't want to go home. Guess there's worse things than fear. I'm glad to know I don't have to be shame about it.

1. After Harriet reassures Celia that she can feel fear and pride at the same time, what does Lennie admit about her own feelings? How does she explain her earlier unkindness?

2. Earlier Celia admitted her fear and her shame at feeling fear. Which feeling does she say is now gone? How has her change in feelings changed her plans?

Now check your answers with your teacher. Review this part of the lesson if you don't understand why an answer was incorrect.

 WRITING ON YOUR OWN 3

In Writing on Your Own 1, you wrote about a problem discussed in the news, and you developed an original character based on a person involved in that problem. In this exercise, you will give your character a voice. Follow these steps:

- Review how you described the problem and the character in Writing on Your Own 1.
- Imagine that, as the problem comes to an end, a news reporter interviews the character. Write questions that you would ask if you were the reporter, such as "Were you frightened during the robbery?" or "Will this accident change your driving habits?" or "How do you think your grandfather feels in the retirement home?" Leave enough space under each question for an answer.
- Answer each question in the voice, or role, of the character. Let the character's words show his or her qualities, feelings, and attitudes—whether they include bravery, cowardice, or meanness.

DISCUSSION GUIDES

1. "Captain Brown," as Harriet refers to John Brown, was hanged for treason against the United States. Yet Harriet thought of him as a great leader and a hero. During the Civil War, one of the patriotic songs of the North stated, "John Brown's body lies a-molderin' in the grave, But his soul keeps marchin' on!" How do you think Brown should be remembered, as a traitor or as a hero? Work with a small group to research the facts of John Brown's life and death and make an objective report to the class. Then class members should discuss the question, presenting reasons for all opinions. At the end of the discussion, take an informal vote on the answer to the question.

2. Before the Civil War, many citizens—both in the North and in the South—agreed that slavery was a major problem, but they couldn't agree upon a solution. What are some of our society's important problems today? What solutions do different groups propose? With your class, discuss which issues you consider most important and which solutions you favor. Try to come up with specific ways in which individuals can become involved in solving the problems.

3. With the class or in a small group, take turns reading the dialogue of *When the Rattlesnake Sounds*. Identify passages that fit these descriptions: humorous, stirring, sad, hopeful.

WRITE A SCENE THAT DEVELOPS A CHARACTER

In earlier assignments in this unit, you developed a character based on a person in the news. In this exercise, you will use what you have learned in these lessons to write a scene that explains your character's personality and feelings.

If you have questions about the writing process, refer to Using the Writing Process (page 261).

- Assemble and review the writing you did for the Writing on Your Own exercises: 1) an introductory note for a play, describing a character based on a real person in the news; 2) a brief scene expressing a character's emotions through stage directions and limited dialogue; 3) an interview with the character.
- Now imagine that the character you developed is applying for a scholarship, loan, or job. Write a scene showing your character interviewing for the scholarship, loan, or job. The only other person in the scene should be the person in authority whom your character must impress. The authority figure should say very little; he or she should mostly ask questions to hear how the applicant thinks and feels. Use the format you have seen in this book to indicate who is speaking. Include stage directions in the scene. Use parentheses before and after the stage directions and underline them to set them apart.
- Invite a classmate to read your scene with you. When you have finished, ask your classmate to tell you what he or she learned about the character through the dialogue and stage directions. Revise the scene as needed to make the character's words and actions more clearly reflect his or her personality.

- Proofread your revised scene for spelling, grammar, punctuation, capitalization, and formatting errors and make sure readers can easily see which character is saying which lines.
- Make a final copy of your scene. If you wish, perform it for the rest of the class before filing it in your portfolio.

Dialogue and Style

I Remember Mama

by John van Druten

Adapted from *Mama's Bank Account* by Kathryn Forbes

INTRODUCTION

The play *I Remember Mama* opened on Broadway in 1944, just a year after the publication of the book it was based on, *Mama's Bank Account.* The success of the play led to a 1948 movie version. Three of the movie's stars were nominated for Academy Awards for their portrayals of Mama, Katrin, and Uncle Chris. The movie, in turn, led to one of the earliest long-running television series about families. *I Remember Mama* was broadcast live every week between July 1949 and July 1956.

The book, play, movie, and television series all tell stories of the adventures of a Norwegian immigrant family in San Francisco in the early 1900s. The stories are recalled by one of the daughters, Katrin Hanson. Papa, a carpenter, works hard to support the family, but there is never any extra money. Mama is the glue that holds the family together through difficult times.

In the excerpt you are about to read, Nels is about 16, Christine and Katrin are between 13 and 15, and Dagmar is eight. Living nearby are Mama's sisters—Jenny, Sigrid, and Trina—and their gruff Uncle Chris, who walks with a limp because of an old injury. Trina wants to get married, like her sisters, but she is afraid to ask Uncle Chris for his approval.

In the scenes leading up to the excerpt, Sigrid complains to Jenny and Trina that without her permission, Uncle Chris has taken her son Arne to the hospital for an operation on an injured knee. Jenny urges both Trina and Sigrid to stand up to Uncle Chris. Meanwhile, Mama learns that Dagmar has a serious ear infection which requires an operation. Uncle Chris, stopping in for a visit, offers to take Dagmar to the hospital in his car. Although he means to be helpful, his take-charge attitude irritates Dagmar's doctor.

Stage directions at the beginning of Act I explain that the curtains, called *travelers*, open on Mama's kitchen in the center of the stage. Shorter scenes, with little in the way of scenery or props, take place on large turntables at either side of the stage, in front of the curtains. While a scene is played on a turntable, the travelers cover the center of the stage, and the scenery there can be changed to the next important setting. At the beginning of this scene, the kitchen has been replaced by the hospital. Notice how later scenes on the turntables keep the action moving forward while the curtains are closed for scenery changes on the main set.

ABOUT THE AUTHOR

Kathryn Forbes was the pen name of Kathryn Anderson McLean (1909–1966). She was born in San Francisco, graduated from high school there, and became a full-time writer of short stories, nonfiction articles, and radio scripts. Her most famous work was *Mama's Bank Account*, a collection of stories loosely based on her own childhood in a Norwegian American family at the turn of the century. The book was dramatized by John van Druten, produced by

Richard Rodgers and Oscar Hammerstein II, and opened on Broadway in 1944 under the title *I Remember Mama*.

John van Druten (1901–1957) was a British-born director and playwright who spent most of his life in the United States. He directed the original production of the Rogers and Hammerstein musical *The King and I*. He also wrote several successful Broadway plays that were later turned into movies, including *I Remember Mama*. Another of his plays, *I Am a Camera*, winner of the Drama Critics Circle Award in 1952, was the basis of the musical *Cabaret*, a hit both on stage and as a movie.

ABOUT THE LESSONS

In the lessons that follow this excerpt, you will look at how the dialogue of a play contributes to its success. The dialogue must develop the plot, which is essential, but it must do much more. For example, dialogue must help establish characters, present themes, and give the play a distinct style. A playwright must select and arrange the characters' words to achieve all these purposes at once. Each playwright does this in a slightly different way for each play. The lessons following this selection will focus on how John van Druten, with the help of Kathryn Forbes's original story, uses dialogue so effectively in this play.

WRITING: DEVELOPING DIALOGUE

Dialogue is the tool that a writer uses to develop the characters, events, and ideas in a play. While watching a play, the audience cannot read lengthy descriptions about the characters' thoughts and feelings, as they can in a novel. So they must rely upon the characters' dialogue to understand what each character is thinking and feeling and planning to do next.

At the end of this unit, you will write dialogue for a scene. The activity below will help you begin thinking about the words and style you might use.

- Think of some situations that have turned out to be troublesome because you've "gotten your wires crossed" with someone. Perhaps you didn't receive a message about a last-minute change of plans, so you showed up at the wrong place or at the wrong time. Maybe you followed the directions someone gave you, but the directions were incorrect so you got there late. List at least three situations that you got into that were caused by honest mistakes.
- Choose one of the situations on your list. Then choose one of these responses to that situation: 1) Get the other person to feel sorry for you and forgive you, or 2) persuade the other person to think he or she was responsible for the mistake and to ask your forgiveness.
- Then make a list of words, phrases, or sentences that you might use in the situation you have chosen.

AS YOU READ

The questions below will help you become aware of the dialogue in *I Remember Mama*. As you read, keep these questions in mind:

- How would you describe the dialogue in this play?
- Is there anything special about the way particular characters speak?
- How do conversations between characters establish and reinforce themes?

I Remember Mama

by John van Druten

Adapted from *Mama's Bank Account* by Kathryn Forbes

CHARACTERS		
Mama	**A Nurse**	
Nels	**Dr. Johnson**	
Aunt Sigrid	**Christine**	
Aunt Trina	**Katrin**	
Aunt Jenny	**Arne**	
Uncle Chris	**Another Nurse**	
Mr. Thorkelson	**Scrubwoman, nurses, and doctors**	

SETTING

The action passes in and around San Francisco some years ago. The period of the play is around 1910.

STAGE

The travelers [curtains] part on a hospital corridor. A main back flat representing the wall, runs diagonally up from the front of the main stage L. *towards the back. Down front* L. *is a bench, on which* **Mama** *and* **Nels** *are sitting, holding hands, looking off.*

Below the bench is the elevator, and above the bench, set back a little, is a closet for brooms and mops, etc. The reception desk, at which a nurse is sitting, is R.C., *toward the front. The wall goes up into darkness, and behind the nurse's desk is darkness.*

As the curtains open, there is a hubbub down front by the nurse's desk, where the **Aunts** *are haranguing*[1] **Uncle Chris.** **Mr. Thorkelson** *stands slightly in back of them.*

Sigrid.   But, Uncle Chris, I tell you I must see him!

Uncle Chris.   *(storming)* You don't understand English? No visitors for twenty-four hours.

Sigrid.   But *you've* seen him.

Uncle Chris.   I am not visitor. I am exception.

Sigrid.   Well, then, his mother should be an exception, too. I'll see the doctor.

Uncle Chris.   *I* have seen doctor. I have told him you are not goot for Arne.

Sigrid.   Not good for my own son. . . .

Uncle Chris.   Not goot at all. You cry over him. I go now. *(He starts to do so, but* **Jenny** *pushes* **Trina** *forward.)*

Trina.   *(with desperate courage)* Uncle Chris . . . Uncle Chris . . . I *must* speak to you.

Uncle Chris.   I have business.

Trina.   But, Uncle Chris. . . . I want to get married.

Uncle Chris.   Well, then, *get* married. *(He starts off again.)*

---

[1] scolding at length

Trina. No, wait, I . . . I want to marry Mr. Thorkelson. Here. (*She produces him from behind her.*) Peter, this is Uncle Chris. Uncle Chris, this is Mr. Thorkelson.

Uncle Chris. (*staring at him*) So?

Mr. Thorkelson. How are you, sir?

Uncle Chris. Busy. (*He turns again.*)

Trina. Please, Uncle Chris. . . .

Uncle Chris. What is? You want to marry him? All right, marry him. I have other things to think about.

Trina. (*eagerly*) Then . . . then you give your permission?

Uncle Chris. Yes, I give my permission. If you want to be a fool, I cannot stop you.

Trina. (*gratefully*) Oh, thank you, Uncle Chris.

Uncle Chris. So. Is all?

Trina. (*anxious to escape*) Yes, I think is all.

Jenny. (*firmly*) No!!

Uncle Chris. No? (**Mr. Thorkelson** *is pushed forward again.*)

Mr. Thorkelson. Well, there . . . there was a little something else. You see, Trina mentioned . . . well, in the old country it was always usual . . . and after all, we do all come from the old country. . . .

Uncle Chris. What is it? What you want?

Mr. Thorkelson. Well, it's a question of Trina's . . . well, not to mince matters . . . her dowry.[2]

Uncle Chris. (*shouting*) Her what?

Mr. Thorkelson. (*very faintly*) Her dowry. . .

Uncle Chris. Ah. Her dowry. Trina wants a dowry. She is forty-two years old. . . .

---

[2] money or property, usually from a woman's parents, that she brings to her husband upon marrying

Trina. (*interrupting*) No, Uncle Chris. . . .

Uncle Chris. (*without pausing*) And it is not enough she gets husband. She must have dowry.

Nurse. (*who has been trying to interrupt, now bangs on her desk*) PLEASE! Would you mind going and discussing your family matters somewhere else? This is a hospital, not a marriage bureau!

Uncle Chris. (*after glaring at the* **Nurse,** *turns to* **Mr. Thorkelson**) You come into waiting room. I talk to you about dowry. (*He strides off into the darkness behind the nurse's desk.* **Mr. Thorkelson,** *with an appealing look back at* **Trina,** *follows him. The Aunts now remember* **Mama,** *sitting on the bench, and cross to her.*)

Jenny. Did you hear that, Marta?

Mama. (*out of a trance*) What?

Jenny. Uncle Chris.

Mama. No, I do not hear. I wait for doctor. Is two hours since they take Dagmar to operating room. More.

Sigrid. Two hours? That's nothing! When Mrs. Bergman had her gall bladder removed she was *six* hours on the table.

Mama. Sigrid, I do not want to hear about Mrs. Bergman. I do not want to hear about anything. I wait for doctor. Please, you go away now. You come this evening.

Trina. But, Marta, you can't stay here all by yourself.

Mama. I have Nels. Please, Trina . . . I wait for doctor . . . you go now.

Jenny. We go.

Trina. Oh, but I must wait for Peter and Uncle Chris. . . .

Jenny. We'll go next door and have some coffee. Sigrid, do you have money?

Sigrid. Yes, I . . . I have a little.

Jenny.   Good. Then I treat you. We'll be next door if you want us, Marta. (**Mama** *nods without looking at them, her eyes still fixed on the elevator door. The* **Aunts** *leave, going down the steps from the stage as though they were the hospital steps, and off* L.

For a moment, the stage is quiet. Then a **Scrubwoman** *enters from down* R., *carrying a mop and pail which she puts into the closet, and then leaves. The elevator door opens and a doctor in white coat comes out, followed by an orderly, carrying a tray of dressings. They disappear up* R. *behind the desk.* **Mama** *rises, agitatedly, looking after them. Then* **Dr. Johnson** *returns from* R. *front, carrying his hat and bag. He sees* **Mama** *and crosses to her,* C.)

Doctor.   Oh, Mrs. Hanson. . . .

Mama.   Doctor. . . .

Doctor.   Well, Dagmar's fine. She came through it beautifully. She's back in bed now, sleeping off the anesthetic.

Mama.   Thank you, Doctor. (*She shakes hands with him.*)

Doctor.   You're very welcome.

Mama.   Is good of you, Doctor. (*She shakes hands with him again.*) Where is she? I go to her now.

Doctor.   Oh, I'm sorry, but I'm afraid that's against the rules. You shall see her tomorrow.

Mama.   Tomorrow? But, Doctor, she is so little. When she wakes she will be frightened.

Doctor.   The nurses will take care of her. Excellent care. You needn't worry. You see, for the first twenty-four hours, clinic patients aren't allowed to see visitors. The wards must be kept quiet.

Mama.   I will not make a sound.

Doctor.   I'm very sorry. Tomorrow. And now . . . (*He glances at his watch.*) Good afternoon. (*He puts on his hat and* *goes out L., down the steps and off.* **Mama** *stands still a moment, looking after him.)*

Mama.   Come, Nels. We go find Dagmar.

Nels.   But, Mama, the doctor said . . .

Mama.   We find Dagmar. (*She looks vaguely around her. Then goes to the nurse's desk.*) You tell me, please, where I can find my daughter?

Nurse.   What name?

Mama.   Dagmar.

Nels.   Dagmar Hanson.

Nurse.   (*looking at her record book*) Hanson, Ward A. Along there. (*She points upstage.* **Mama** *starts to go up.*) Oh, just a moment. (**Mama** *returns.*) When did she come in?

Mama.   This morning. They just finish operation.

Nurse.   Oh, well, then I'm afraid you can't see her today. No visitors for the first twenty-four hours.

Mama.   Am not visitor. I am her Mama.

Nurse.   I'm sorry, but it's against the rules.

Mama.   Just for one minute. Please.

Nurse.   I'm sorry. It's against the rules. (**Mama** *stands staring.* **Nels** *touches her arm. She looks at him, nods, trying to smile, then turns and walks with him to L. and down the steps.*)

Mama.   We must think of some way.

Nels.   Mama, they'll let you see her tomorrow. They said so.

Mama.   If I don't see her today how will I know that all is well with her? What can I tell Papa when he comes home from work?

Nels.   The nurses will look after her, Mama. Would you like to come next door for some coffee?

Mama. *(shaking her head)* We go home. We have coffee at home. But I must see Dagmar today. *(She plods off* L. *with* **Nels**. *The travelers close. Spot goes up on* R. *turntable.* **Uncle Chris** *and* **Mr. Thorkelson** *are seated on a bench and chair, as in a waiting-room. A table with a potted plant is between them. A clock on the wall points to 2:30.)*

Uncle Chris. Well, it comes then to this. You love my niece, Trina? (**Mr. Thorkelson**, *very scared, gulps and nods.)* You want to marry her? (**Mr. Thorkelson** *nods again.)* You are in position to support her? (**Mr. Thorkelson** *nods again.)* Why, then, you want dowry? *(No answer. He shouts.)* What for you want dowry?

Mr. Thorkelson. Well . . . well, it would be a nice help. And it is customary.

Uncle Chris. Is not customary. Who give dowries? Parents. Why? Because they are so glad they will not have to support their daughters any more, they pay money. I do not support Trina. I do not care if Trina gets married. Why then should I pay to have her married?

Mr. Thorkelson. I never thought of it like that.

Uncle Chris. Is insult to girl to pay dowry. If I do not give dowry, will you still marry Trina?

Mr. Thorkelson. I . . . I don't know.

Uncle Chris. You don't know? You don't know?? You think I let Trina marry a man who will not take her without dowry?

Mr. Thorkelson. No, I suppose you wouldn't.

Uncle Chris. What kind of man would that be? I ask you, what kind of man would that be?

Mr. Thorkelson. *(fascinated—helpless)* Well, not a very nice kind of man.

Uncle Chris. And are you that kind of man?

Mr. Thorkelson. I . . . I don't think so.

Uncle Chris. *(conclusively)* Then you don't want dowry!!

Mr. Thorkelson. *(giving up)* No, I . . . I guess I don't.

Uncle Chris. *(slapping his back)* Goot. Goot. You are goot man. I like you. I give you my blessing. And I send you vedding present. I send you box of oranges! *(While he is boisterously[3] shaking **Mr. Thorkelson**'s hand, blackout. Turntable revolves out.)*

*(The curtains open on the kitchen. It is empty. **Mama** and **Nels** come up the hill from the L. and let themselves into the house. There is silence as they take off their hats and coats.)*

Mama. *(after a moment)* Where are the girls?

Nels. I guess they're upstairs. *(goes to door back L. and calls)* Chris! Katrin!

Girls' Voices. Coming!

Nels. Shall I make you some coffee? *(**Mama** shakes her head.)* You said you'd have coffee when you got home.

Mama. Later. First I must think.

Nels. Mama, please don't worry like that. Dagmar's all right. You know she's all right. *(The **Girls** come in back L.)*

Christine. *(trying to be casual)* Well, Mama, everything all right?

Mama. *(nodding)* Is all right. You have eaten?

Katrin. Yes, Mama.

Mama. You drink your milk?

Christine. Yes, Mama.

Mama. Is good.

Christine. *(seeing her face)* Mama, something's the matter.

Katrin. *(over-dramatically)* Mama, Dagmar's not—? She isn't—? Mama!

Mama. No, Dagmar is fine. The doctor say she is fine. *(She rises.)* What is time?

---

[3] noisily and roughly.

Nels.   It's three o'clock.

Mama.   Three hours till Papa come. (*She looks around and then goes slowly into the pantry, back* R.)

Katrin.   Nels, what is it? There *is* something the matter.

Nels.   They wouldn't let Mama see Dagmar. It's a rule of the hospital.

Christine.   But Dagmar's all right?

Nels.   Oh, yes, she's all right.

Christine.   (*impatiently*) Well, then . . . !

Nels.   But Mama's very upset. She started talking to me in Norwegian in the street-car.

Katrin.   (*emotionally*) What can we do?

Christine.   (*coldly*) You can't do anything. When will they let her see Dagmar?

Nels.   Tomorrow.

Christine.   Well, then, we'll just have to wait till tomorrow.

Katrin.   Chris, how can you be so callous! Can't you see that Mama's heart is breaking?

Christine.   No, I can't. And you can't, either. People's hearts don't break.

Katrin.   They do, too.

Christine.   Only in books. (**Mama** *comes back; she wears an apron, and carries a scrub brush and a bucket of hot water.*) Why, Mama, what are you going to do?

Mama.   I scrub the floor. (*She gets down on her knees.*)

Christine.   But you scrubbed it yesterday.

Mama.   I scrub it again. (*She starts to do so.*)

Katrin.   But, Mama . . .

Mama.   (*bending low*) Comes a time when you've got to get down on your knees.

Katrin.   (*to* **Christine**) Now do you believe me? (**Christine**, *suddenly unendurably moved, turns and rushes from the room.*)

Nels.   Mama, don't. Please don't. You must be tired.

Katrin.   *(strangely)* Let her alone, Nels. *(They stand in silence watching* **Mama** *scrub. Suddenly she stops.)* What is it, Mama? What is it?

Mama.   *(sitting back on her haunches)* I think of something! *(slowly)* I think I think of something! *(The lights dim and the curtains close on the kitchen.)*

(From down front L. **Uncle Chris**'s *voice singing. The lights slowly come up on the* L. *turntable, showing* **Arne**, *a child of about eight, in a hospital bed, with* **Uncle Chris** *beside him.)*

Uncle Chris.   *(singing)*

"Ten t'ousand Svedes vent t'rough de veeds

At de battle of Coppen-hagen.

Ten t'ousand Svedes vent t'rough de veeds

Chasing vun Nor-ve-gan!"

Arne.   Uncle Chris!

Uncle Chris.   Yes, Arne?

Arne.   Uncle Chris, does it *have* to hurt like this?

Uncle Chris.   If you vant it to be vell, and not to valk always like Uncle Chris, it does . . . for a little. Is very bad?

Arne.   It is . . . kinda. . . . Oo-oo . . .!

Uncle Chris.   Arne, don't you know any svear vords?

Arne.   W-what?

Uncle Chris.   Don't you know any svear vords?

Arne.   N-no, Uncle Chris. Not real ones.

Uncle Chris.   Then I tell you two fine vons to use when pain is bad. Are "Darn" and "Darnit." You say them?

Arne.   N-now?

Uncle Chris.   No, not now. When pain comes again. You say them then. They help plenty. I know. I haf pain, too. I say them all the time. And if pain is *very* bad, you say, "Goshdarnit." But only if is *very* bad. Is bad now?

Arne.   No, it's . . . it's a little better.

Uncle Chris.   You sleep some now, maybe?

Arne.   I'll try. Will . . . will you stay here, Uncle Chris?

Uncle Chris.   Sure. Sure. I stay here. You are not frightened of Uncle Chris?

Arne.   No. Not any more.

Uncle Chris.   Goot. Goot. You like I sing some more?

Arne.   If you wouldn't mind. But maybe something a little . . . well, quieter.

Uncle Chris.   *(tenderly)* Sure. Sure. *(He begins quietly to sing a Norwegian lullaby; in the midst,* **Arne** *cries out.)*

Arne.   Oo-oo. . . . Oh, *darn.* Darn. Goshdarnit!

Uncle Chris.   *(delighted)* Goot! It helps—eh?

Arne.   *(with pleased surprise)* Yes—yes.

Uncle Chris.   Then you sleep some! *(He fixes* **Arne***'s pillows for him, and resumes the lullaby, seated on his chair beside the bed. After another verse, he leans over, assuring himself that the child is asleep and then very quietly, without interrupting his singing, takes a flask from his pocket and lifts it to his lips, as the light dims. The table revolves out.)*

(The curtains part on the hospital corridor again. There is a different **Nurse** *now at the reception desk, talking on the telephone as* **Mama** *and* **Katrin** *come in from L. and up the steps.)*

Mama.   *(as they come up, in an undertone)* Is not the same nurse. Katrin, you take my hat and coat. *(She takes them off, revealing that she still wears her apron.)*

Katrin.   But, Mama, won't they . . .

Mama.   *(interrupting, finger to lips)* Ssh! You let me go ahead. You wait on bench for me. *(She goes to the closet door above the bench and opens it.* **Katrin** *stares after her in*

---

[4] fearful anxiety

trepidation.[4] **Mama** *takes out a damp mop and pail, and gets down on her knees in front of the nurse's desk, starting to clean the floor. The* **Nurse** *looks up.* **Mama** *catches her eye.)*

Mama. *(brightly)* Very dirty floors.

Nurse. Yes, I'm glad they've finally decided to clean them. Aren't you working late?

Mama. *(quickly, lowering her head)* Floors need cleaning. *(She pushes her way, crawling on hands and knees, up behind the desk, and disappears up the corridor, still scrubbing.* **Katrin** *steals to the bench, where she sits, still clutching* **Mama**'s *hat and coat, looking interestedly around her. The light dims, leaving her in a single spot, as she starts to talk to herself.)*

Katrin. *(to herself)* "The Hospital" . . . A poem by Katrin Hanson. *(She starts to improvise.)*

"She waited, fearful, in the hall,

And held her bated breath."

Breath—yes, that'll rhyme with death. *(She repeats the first two lines.)*

"She waited fearful in the hall

And held her bated breath.

She trembled at the least footfall,

And kept her mind on death."

(She gets a piece of paper and pencil from her pocket and begins to scribble, as a **Nurse** *comes out of the elevator, carrying some charts, which she takes to the desk, and then goes out down* R. **Katrin** *goes on with her poem.)*

"Ah, God, 'twas agony to wait.

To wait and watch and wonder. . . ."

Wonder—under—bunder—funder—sunder.[5] Sunder! *(nods to herself and goes on again)*

"To wait and watch and wonder,

---

[5] break apart

About her infant sister's fate,

If Death life's bonds would sunder."

(*then to herself again, looking front.*) That's beautiful. Yes, but it isn't true. Dagmar isn't dying. It's funny—I don't want her to die—and yet when Mama said she was all right, I was almost—well, almost disappointed. It wasn't exciting any more. Maybe Christine's right, and I haven't any heart. How awful! "The girl without a heart." That'd be a nice title for a story. "The girl without a heart sat in the hospital corridor. . . ." (*The lights come up again as* **Uncle Chris** *appears, up* R. *behind the desk. He wears his hat and is more than a little drunk. He sees* **Katrin.**)

Uncle Chris.   Katrinë! What you do here? (*He sits on the bench beside her.*)

Katrin.   (*nervously*) I'm waiting for Mama.

Uncle Chris.   Where is she?

Katrin.   (*scared*) I . . . I don't know.

Uncle Chris.   What you mean . . . you don't know?

Katrin.   (*whispering*) I think . . . I think she's seeing Dagmar.

Uncle Chris.   (*shaking his head*) Is first day. They do not allow visitors first day.

Katrin.   (*trying to make him aware of the* **Nurse**) I know. But I think that's where she is.

Uncle Chris.   Where *is* Dagmar?

Katrin.   I don't know. (**Uncle Chris** *rises and goes to the* **Nurse** *at the desk.*)

Uncle Chris.   In what room is my great-niece, Dagmar Hanson?

Nurse.   (*looking at her book*) Hanson . . . Hanson . . . when did she come in?

Uncle Chris.   This morning.

Nurse. Oh yes. Were you wanting to see her?

Uncle Chris. What room is she in?

Nurse. I asked were you wanting to see her.

Uncle Chris. And *I* ask what room she is in.

Nurse. We don't allow visitors the first day.

Uncle Chris. Have I said I vant to visit her? I ask what room she is in.

Nurse. Are you by any chance, Mr. . . . *(looking at her book)* Halvorsen?

Uncle Chris. *(proudly, and correcting her pronunciation)* Christopher Halvorsen.

Nurse. Did you say you were her uncle?

Uncle Chris. Her great-uncle.

Nurse. Well, then, I'm afraid I can't tell you anything about her.

Uncle Chris. Why not?

Nurse. Orders.

Uncle Chris. Whose orders?

Nurse. Dr. Johnson's. There's a special note here. Patient's uncle, Mr. Halvorsen, not to be admitted or given information under any circumstances.

Uncle Chris. *(after a moment's angry stupefaction[6])* Goshdarnit! *(He strides away down* L. *taking out his flask, and shaking it, only to find it empty. Mama returns from up* R., *carrying the mop and pail, walking now, and smiling trumphantly.)*

Mama. *(to the* **Nurse***)* Thank you. *(She replaces the mop and pail in the closet, and then sees* **Uncle Chris.***)* Uncle Chris, Dagmar is fine!

Uncle Chris. *(coming back to her, amazed)* You see her?

Mama. Sure, Uncle Chris, I see her.

---

[6] stunned amazement

Uncle Chris. *(reiterating,[7] incredulous[8])* You see Dagmar?!

Mama. Sure. *(She takes her hat from **Katrin** and starts to put it on.)* Is fine hospital. But such floors! A mop is never good. Floors should be scrubbed with a brush. We go home. Uncle Chris, you come with us? I make coffee.

Uncle Chris. Pah! Vot good is coffee? I go get drink.

Mama. *(reprovingly[9])* Uncle Chris!

Uncle Chris. Marta, you are fine voman. Fine. But I go get drink.

Mama. *(quickly aside to **Katrin**)* His leg hurts him.

Uncle Chris. And you do not make excuses for me! I get drunk because I like it.

Mama. *(conciliating[10] him)* Sure, Uncle Chris.

Uncle Chris. *(shouting)* I like it! *(then, with a change)* No, is not true. You know is not true. I do not like to get drunk at all. But I do not like to come home with you, either. *(growing slightly maudlin[11])* You have family. Is fine thing. You do not know how fine. Katrinë, one day when you grow up, maybe you know what a fine thing family is. I haf no family.

Katrin. But, Uncle Chris, Mama's always said you were the *head* of the family.

Uncle Chris. Sure. Sure. I am head of the family, but I haf no family. So I go get drunk. You understand, Marta?

Mama. Sure, Uncle Chris. You go get drunk. *(sharply)* But don't you feel sorry for yourself! (**Uncle Chris** *glares at her a moment, then strides off* R., *boisterously singing his song of*

---

[7] repeating

[8] unbelieving

[9] in a manner expressing disapproval

[10] soothing the anger of

[11] tearfully sentimental

"Ten Thousand Swedes." **Mama** *watches him go, then takes her coat from* **Katrin**.*)* Is fine man. Has fine ideas about family. (**Katrin** *helps her on with her coat.*) I can tell Papa now that Dagmar is fine. She wake while I am with her. I explain rules to her. She will not expect us now until tomorrow afternoon.

Katrin. You won't try and see her again before that?

Mama. *(gravely)* No. That would be against the rules! Come. We go home.

(They go off L.*)*

CURTAIN

REVIEWING AND INTERPRETING

Record your answers to these questions in your personal literature notebook. Follow the directions for each part.

REVIEWING   Try to complete each of these sentences without looking back at the selection.

Identifying Cause   **1.** At the hospital, Mr. Thorkelson asks Uncle Chris for
and Effect   Trina's dowry because
                            a. he feels that Uncle Chris should pay him to marry Trina.
                            b. he doesn't really love Trina and just wants her money.
                            c. Jenny pushes him into demanding it.
                            d. the hospital is as good a place as any for the discussion.

Identifying Sequence   **2.** Just before figuring out how to get into Dagmar's room,
                              Mama
                            a. talks with Uncle Chris.
                            b. goes home with Nels.
                            c. gets the doctor's report about Dagmar.
                            d. begins to scrub the kitchen floor.

Understanding   **3.** While Katrin writes her poem in the hospital, she realizes
Main Ideas   that
                            a. both she and her poem are overly dramatic.
                            b. Dagmar is likely to die.
                            c. it's often difficult to find a good rhyme.
                            d. it's a good thing she brought her pencil.

Recalling Facts   **4.** While she waits, Katrin is worried that
                            a. Mama will be caught breaking the hospital rule.
                            b. Dagmar will die of her ear infection.
                            c. Uncle Chris will get into trouble for drinking at the
                               hospital.
                            d. she will leave her homework in the hospital waiting
                               area.

Understanding the
Elements of a Play
(Staging)

5. The passage of time between scenes is sometimes shown by
   a. dimming the lights and raising them a few minutes later.
   b. putting a spotlight on a clock on the stage.
   c. having the actors and actresses appear in old-fashioned clothes.
   d. having Uncle Chris sing between scenes.

INTERPRETING   To complete these sentences, you may look back at the selection if you'd like.

Analyzing

6. The best way to describe Uncle Chris is that he is
   a. a worthless drunk.
   b. a complex person who hides his problems with noisy, showy talk.
   c. a cruel person who doesn't like other people at all.
   d. usually a gracious person who, at times, loses his temper with his nieces.

Making Inferences

7. The way the author depicts Nels, Christine, and Katrin shows that they
   a. are usually behavior problems in school.
   b. are caring and family-oriented.
   c. all get good grades in school.
   d. are jealous of Dagmar and the attention she gets.

Predicting Outcomes

8. The next time Mama visits the hospital,
   a. she'll tell the nurse how she fooled everyone.
   b. the doctor still won't let her see Dagmar.
   c. she'll find Uncle Chris teaching Dagmar to swear.
   d. she will behave as if nothing unusual happened.

Making
Generalizations

9. Both Mama and Uncle Chris believe that when you have troubles,
   a. you can forget your problems by drinking.
   b. you need to take action and avoid feeling sorry for yourself.
   c. you can count on the kindness of strangers to take care of you.
   d. you should rely on people in authority and do everything they say.

Understanding the
Elements of a Play
(Characters)

10. From the scenes in this excerpt, it appears that the three most important characters in the play are
   a. Jenny, Sigrid, and Trina.
   b. Uncle Chris, Mama, and Mr. Thorkelson.
   c. Uncle Chris, Mama, and Katrin.
   d. Uncle Chris, Mama, and Dagmar.

Now check your answers with your teacher. Study the questions you answered incorrectly. What types of questions were they? Talk with your teacher about ways to work on those skills.

Dialogue and Style

In the production of a play, the scenery and costumes can communicate the setting and mood of the play. The actors' movements on stage and their delivery of their lines can reveal the characters' personalities. However, dialogue is the playwright's main tool to communicate the characters' ideas and feelings to an audience. Through their words, the characters explain themselves and their problems. They make the audience understand why their problems are important.

When you read a play, you miss out on elaborate scenery, colorful costumes, and dramatic acting. However, with your imagination to fill in these details, you have the one necessary element of the play: the dialogue. The only special effects that a play really needs are carefully chosen words. It is the quality of the dialogue that makes or breaks a play.

In the lessons that follow, you will look at a few of the ways in which playwright John van Druten puts dialogue to work:

1. He uses dialogue to develop the characters by giving them distinctive ways of speaking and using words.

2. He uses dialogue to develop the theme by having different characters consider the same topic at different times and from different viewpoints.

3. He uses the characters' language to give the whole play a distinctive tone and style.

LESSON 1 — HOW CHARACTERS SPEAK AND USE WORDS

In real life, no two people speak exactly the same. Even when they express the same idea, two people will speak at different rates of speed and volume, choose different words, and arrange those words differently. If the characters in a play are going to sound believable, the writer must avoid having them all sound alike. The dialogue must include differences that reflect the distinct background and personality of each speaker.

Read this dialogue between Mr. Thorkelson and Uncle Chris. How does Uncle Chris's use of English differ from Mr. Thorkelson's? What can you guess about each character from his use of English?

Uncle Chris. What for you want dowry?

Mr. Thorkelson. Well . . . well, it would be a nice help. And it is customary.

Uncle Chris. Is not customary. Who give dowries? Parents. Why? Because they are so glad they will not have to support their daughters any more, they pay money. I do not support Trina. I do not care if Trina gets married. Why then should I pay to have her married?

Mr. Thorkelson. I never thought of it like that.

Uncle Chris. Is insult to girl to pay dowry. If I do not give dowry, will you still marry Trina?

Mr. Thorkelson. I . . . I don't know.

Uncle Chris. You don't know? You don't know?? You think I let Trina marry a man who will not take her without dowry?

Mr. Thorkelson. No, I suppose you wouldn't.

Uncle Chris. What kind of man would that be? I ask you, what kind of man would that be?

Mr. Thorkelson. *(fascinated—helpless)* Well, not a very nice kind of man.

Note how in the above passage, in any sentence that would contain the word *it* as its subject, Uncle Chris simply skips the subject. He also tends to leave out the articles *a, an,* and *the*. Further, he occasionally arranges his words in a pattern that is not typical of English, as in "What for you want dowry?" Although he has not mastered the language, he uses it forcefully. He not only makes himself understood, he outmaneuvers Mr. Thorkelson, who has a better grasp of the language. Uncle Chris's style of speaking reveals his character as a man who doesn't let his shortcomings get in his way.

In addition to a foreign-sounding arrangement of words, the playwright gives Uncle Chris a Norwegian accent and pronunciation. Note how the spelling in this speech gives the actor—and readers—a hint of how Uncle Chris pronounces his *d*'s and *w*'s:

Uncle Chris. *(slapping his back)* Goot. Goot. You are goot man. I like you. I give you my blessing. And I send you vedding present. I send you box of oranges!

EXERCISE 1

Read this conversation between Mama and her sisters. Then use what you have learned in this lesson to answer the questions that follow.

Jenny. Did you hear that, Marta?

Mama. *(out of a trance)* What?

Jenny. Uncle Chris.

Mama. No, I do not hear. I wait for doctor. Is two hours since they take Dagmar to operating room. More.

Sigrid. Two hours? That's nothing! When Mrs. Bergman had her gall bladder removed she was *six* hours on the table.

Mama. Sigrid, I do not want to hear about Mrs. Bergman. I do not want to hear about anything. I wait for doctor. Please, you go away now. You come this evening.

Trina.   But, Marta, you can't stay here all by yourself.

Mama.   I have Nels. Please, Trina . . . I wait for doctor . . . you go now.

Jenny.   We go.

Trina.   Oh, but I must wait for Peter and Uncle Chris. . . .

Jenny.   We'll go next door and have some coffee. . . .

1. Compare Mama's use of English with that of her sisters. From the way they all speak, which of the four sisters do you suppose lived the longest time in Norway? Give reasons for your answer.

2. Despite the shortness of this scene, the dialogue brings out some clear differences in style and attitude among the four sisters. Which of the four sisters is the most inclined to take charge? Which is most likely to persist in what she feels is important, despite others' opinions? Which is the most timid? Point out lines that support each of your answers.

Now check your answers with your teacher. Review this part of the lesson if you don't understand why an answer was incorrect.

WRITING ON YOUR OWN 1

In this exercise you will use what you have learned in this lesson to recreate the speech of a real person. Follow these steps.

• Choose a person or character that you know well or have seen often on television—for example, a newscaster or a character in a regular series. You should recognize some difference between the way you speak and the way that person or character speaks. For example, the person may use jargon that you barely understand, let alone use, such as terms about computers, sports, or music. Perhaps the person uses a different dialect or has an accent. Or the person may often use more difficult vocabulary or longer sentences than you do. List the differences, and if possible, give an example of each.

- Recall a conversation that you had with a friend recently. Now replay that same conversation in your mind, only replace yourself with your chosen person or character. Think about how your chosen person or character would have expressed your ideas to your friend.

- Write a revised version of the conversation. Record what your friend said just as you remember it. But when you write the ideas that you expressed, use words and sentences that sound not like you but like your chosen person or character.

- Without explaining your changes, have your friend read your account of the conversation. Then ask your friend if he or she notices anything different about your style of talking in that account. If your friend says the revised version of your comments sounds pretty much like you normally do, you have not achieved your goal. Your friend should note that the revised version doesn't accurately reflect what you said or the way you said it.

LESSON 2 — HOW DIALOGUE BUILDS THEME

At the point where this excerpt begins, the plot of *I Remember Mama* has several problems going on. Trina wants to marry and get a dowry, but she is afraid to talk to Uncle Chris. Arne has just had a knee operation, and his mother, Sigrid, is angry with Uncle Chris for consenting to the operation without her permission. Dagmar has just undergone an operation on her ear. Katrin is struggling to become a writer. Do any of the story lines focus on common concerns? Does the playwright develop any message, or theme, by bringing out such a common concern in the dialogue?

We can discover some themes by comparing phrases and topics of apparently unrelated conversations. Examine, for example, the two conversations below. In the first one, Uncle Chris is talking to Arne; in the second one, he is asking the nurse on hall duty for information about Dagmar. Notice how a single word links the conversations.

Arne. Uncle Chris, does it *have* to hurt like this?

Uncle Chris. If you vant it to be vell, and not to valk always like Uncle Chris, it does . . . for a little. Is very bad?

Arne. It is . . . kinda. . . . Oo—oo . . .!

Uncle Chris. Arne, don't you know any svear vords?

Arne. W-what?

Uncle Chris. Don't you know any svear vords?

Arne. N-no, Uncle Chris. Not real ones.

Uncle Chris. Then I tell you two fine vons to use when pain is bad. Are "Darn" and "Darnit." You say them?

Arne. N-now?

Uncle Chris. No, not now. When pain comes again. You say them then. They help plenty. I know. I haf pain, too. I say them all the time. And if pain is *very* bad, you say, "*Gosh*darnit." But only if is *very* bad. Is bad now?

Nurse. Did you say you were her uncle?

Uncle Chris. Her great-uncle.

Nurse. Well, then, I'm afraid I can't tell you anything about her.

Uncle Chris. Why not?

Nurse. Orders.

Uncle Chris.   Whose orders?

Nurse.   Dr. Johnson's. There's a special note here. Patient's uncle, Mr. Halvorsen, not to be admitted or given information under any circumstances.

Uncle Chris.   (*after a moment's angry stupefaction*) Goshdarnit!

The playwright's use of Uncle Chris's special "svear vord" serves two purposes: it focuses attention on the theme of how to handle pain, and it provides insight into Uncle Chris's distress at being stopped cold.

EXERCISE 2

Read and compare the following two excerpts. The first excerpt is from the first scene in the selection, in which Sigrid and Uncle Chris argue about Arne. The second is from the final scene involving Katrin, Uncle Chris, and Mama. Use what you have learned to answer the questions that follow the excerpts.

Sigrid.   But, Uncle Chris, I tell you I must see him!

Uncle Chris.   (*storming*) You don't understand English? No visitors for twenty-four hours.

Sigrid.   But *you've* seen him.

Uncle Chris.   I am not visitor. I am exception.

Sigrid.   Well, then, his mother should be an exception, too. I'll see the doctor.

Uncle Chris.   *I* have seen doctor. I have told him you are not goot for Arne.

Sigrid.   Not good for my own son. . . .

Uncle Chris.   Not goot at all. You cry over him. I go now.

Uncle Chris.   Marta, you are fine voman. Fine. But I go get drink.

Mama.   (*quickly aside to* **Katrin**) His leg hurts him.

Uncle Chris.   And you do not make excuses for me! I get drunk because I like it.

Mama.   (*conciliating*) Sure, Uncle Chris.

Uncle Chris.   (*shouting*) I like it! (*then, with a change*) No, is not true. You know is not true. I do not like to get drunk at all. But I do not like to come home with you, either. (*growing slightly maudlin*) You have family. Is fine thing. You do not know how fine. Katrinë, one day when you grow up, maybe you know what a fine thing family is. I haf no family.

Katrin.   But, Uncle Chris, Mama's always said you were the *head* of the family.

Uncle Chris.   Sure. Sure. I am head of the family, but I haf no family. So I go get drunk. You understand, Marta?

Mama.   Sure, Uncle Chris. You go get drunk. (*sharply*) But don't you feel sorry for yourself!

1. Why did Uncle Chris object to Sigrid's demand to see her son? How did Mama criticize Uncle Chris? What do the two situations have in common?

2. In your own words, state the theme that the playwright suggests in the dialogue of these two scenes.

Now check your answers with your teacher. Review this part of the lesson if you don't understand why an answer was incorrect.

WRITING ON YOUR OWN 2

In this exercise you will select a theme to develop in the scene you will write. Follow these steps:

- Recall some sayings that have to do with mistakes or avoiding mistakes, such as "There's no use crying over spilt milk" and "Measure twice, cut once." List as many sayings as you can.
- Then think of ideas that you would like to express about mistakes—avoiding them, recovering from them, learning from them, and so on. Think of at least three different ideas and state them in your own words. Add them to your list.
- Choose the statement from your list that you agree with most strongly. At the end of this unit, you will write a scene that develops the statement's message.

LESSON 3   DIALOGUE AND STYLE

When discussing a writer's style, we look at how he or she uses words to build sentences and ideas. We find answers to questions such as these:

Words—Are the words short and familiar, or long and exotic? Are most of them nouns and verbs? Or does the writer use many describing words, both adjectives and adverbs?

Sentences—Are most of the sentences short and simple, each having a single subject and predicate? Or are they long and complex, made up of complicated phrases or ideas?

Content—Do the sentences use figures of speech, such as similes, metaphors, and symbols? Does the writer make logical, direct connections between ideas or develop ideas in a more roundabout fashion?

Tone—Is the tone of the writing conversational? dramatic? unnatural? confused?

Mood—Is the mood humorous or serious? something else? Do the scenes move at a fast or slow pace?

One of the most prominent characteristics of *I Remember Mama* is the natural sound of the dialogue. All of the characters use familiar words. They speak in short sentences or phrases, as most of us do in real life. In normal conversations, we don't usually take time to state our ideas in long, carefully constructed sentences. In fact, we often don't finish our sentences at all if we notice that our listeners already understand our point or have lost interest. Notice how these speakers leave thoughts unfinished:

Sigrid.   Not good for my own son. . . .

Nels.   But, Mama, the doctor said . . .

Katrin.   (*over-dramatically*) Mama, Dagmar's not—? She isn't—? Mama!

Christine.   (*impatiently*) Well, then . . . !

Arne.   It is . . . kinda. . . . Oo—oo . . .!

Katrin.   But, Mama, won't they . . .

There is evidence to show that the playwright consciously kept sentences short and simple to match the style of real conversations. One of the longest phrases in the selection is this one: "Patient's uncle, Mr. Halvorsen, not to be admitted or given information under any circumstances." Ironically, the nurse is repeating the note that Dr. Johnson left in writing.

EXERCISE 3

Review the entire excerpt from *I Remember Mama*, keeping in mind the writer's style. Then use what you have learned in this lesson to answer the following questions.

1. Describe the pacing of the play. Do the scenes generally have fast-paced action, or are they slower moving? Do they take time to develop the characters and situations, or

do they hurry from one funny line or exciting moment to the next?

2. Which of the words in the following list would you use to describe the tone of the play? Choose all that apply and explain your choices.

bitter   sharp   scornful   vulgar   hard-hitting
loving   warm   amusing   moody   respectful

Now check your answers with your teacher. Review this part of the lesson if you don't understand why an answer was incorrect.

WRITING ON YOUR OWN ⬚3⬚

What is your usual writing style? Do you have one? To find out, first collect three or more papers that you have written within the past few months. Then follow these steps:

- Review the questions listed in Lesson 3 concerning the elements that contribute to a writer's style. Reread your writing with those questions in mind. Look for similarities among all your pieces of writing.
- Write a short paragraph describing your own writing style. Again, keep the questions from the lesson in mind as you report your answers. Describe the types of words you use, the length of your sentences, whether you use humor, and so on.

DISCUSSION GUIDES

1. Was the hospital right in enforcing its rules without exceptions, or should Mama have been allowed to see Dagmar right after surgery? Are there situations where rules cause more trouble than they prevent? Prepare arguments for one side of this issue or the other. Then, with a partner, debate the issue with two students who take the opposite side. Ask an audience to decide which pair presented the stronger argument.

2. Katrin admits that when her sister was out of danger she felt disappointed because "it wasn't exciting anymore." Have you ever had that feeling? Why do you suppose people like excitement, even when there are negative results? Discuss this question with your classmates. Can you come up with some possible answers?

3. In this play, the characters recognize that the practice of a bride bringing a dowry into the marriage is not usually a part of modern American culture. Can you think of any traditions that immigrants have brought to the United States that have become part of our culture? Are there situations where practicing traditions from the "old country" would be problematic in America? Discuss these issues with your classmates. Use specific incidents and examples to illustrate your points.

WRITE DIALOGUE FOR A SCENE

In this unit you have examined how dialogue can develop characters by indicating different speech patterns and how it develops themes by bringing up a topic repeatedly over the course of a selection. You also have examined elements of style. Now you will use what you have learned to write dialogue for a scene that develops a character and a theme and that also has a certain intentional style.

If you have questions about the writing process, refer to Using the Writing Process (page 261).

- Assemble the work you did for the writing exercises in this unit. You should have the following: 1) an account of a conversation you had, revised to have a different speaker express your ideas; 2) a list of possible themes, from which you chose one to develop; 3) an analysis of your usual writing style.

- Choose a situation involving a mistake. If you'd like, use one of the personal experiences that you listed for the writing exercise at the beginning of this unit.

- Choose two characters to appear in your scene. One may sound like you. The other must sound noticeably different. If you'd like, use the speaker you developed for the exercise in Writing on Your Own 1.

- Write a short scene about the mistake. Include dialogue that presents the message you chose during the Writing on Your Own 2 exercise. Try to have both of the characters say something on that topic in their own words, not the words you used for the earlier exercise. Use the format you have seen in the plays throughout this book.

- Invite a classmate to read the scene aloud with you. Then have your classmate tell you if he or she recognized the differences between the speakers and was aware of the theme. Revise the scene as needed to make these qualities clearer.

- Proofread your scene for spelling, grammar, punctuation, capitalization, and formatting errors.
- Make a final copy and save it in your writing portfolio. If possible, you and some classmates may wish to present your scene to the class.

Setting

The Monkey's Paw

by W. W. Jacobs

Adapted by Harriet Dexter

INTRODUCTION

ABOUT THE SELECTION

Mr. and Mrs. White and their adult son Herbert are fascinated by the tales that Sergeant-Major Morris has brought back from India. The Whites are entertaining Morris at their cottage in England when he shows them a particularly interesting item—a monkey's paw. Morris explains that an Indian holy man put a spell on the paw many years ago. According to Morris, whoever owns the paw can have three wishes. However, the way the wishes are granted will prove that fate rules people's lives, and that it is dangerous to interfere with fate.

At first the Whites take the story lightly, not believing the paw could have any special abilities. But soon they find that they can no longer joke about the paw and its power.

ABOUT THE AUTHOR

W. W. Jacobs (1863–1943) was born in London, England. Because his father was a dock manager, Jacobs spent his childhood roaming the wharves and shipyards of London and hearing stories about the sea. He later used these tales in his writing. Jacobs did not become a writer early in life. Instead, he worked for many years as a clerk with the savings bank department of the post office. He always dreamed of becoming a writer, though. Soon after his first book—a collection of sea stories called *Many Cargoes*—became an immediate success, he gave up his job as a postal worker and began a full-time writing career. Jacobs wrote in a variety of forms, including short stories, novels, and plays. His works range from sea adventures and humorous stories to grim horror tales.

Harriet Dexter skillfully transformed Mr. Jacobs's popular short story, "The Monkey's Paw," into a stage play. It first appeared in *Plays* magazine in 1983.

WRITING: DEVELOPING A SETTING

At the end of this unit, you will create a setting for the opening scene of a play. You will describe what the audience sees as the curtain rises. The suggestions below will help you get started:

- Look around you, wherever you are sitting. List some of the objects that surround you.
- Review your list of objects. If you were to try to recreate the room you are in, what would be the most important objects to include? Mark a check next to those objects.
- Now look at the light in the room. Is it a bright fluorescent light? Is the room lit by sunlight? Is it mostly dark and lit only by a single lightbulb? List a few words or phrases that describe the room's lighting.
- Add any last details to your lists, and then store them in your writing portfolio. You will use them later in the unit.

ABOUT THE LESSONS

The lessons that follow *The Monkey's Paw* focus on the setting of a play, that is, when and where it takes place. The setting is usually described in stage directions throughout the play. In some cases, the setting also may be revealed by what the characters say and do. The playwright chooses just the right setting to present his or her story. As the curtain rises, the first view of the setting prepares the audience for the story that is about to unfold. As the play progresses, the setting may change, reflecting important changes in the characters and the plot.

AS YOU READ

The following questions will help you understand the playwright's use of setting. Think about the questions as you read *The Monkey's Paw*.

• How does the setting affect your mood as you read this play?
• How does the setting help to explain the characters and their actions?
• How does the setting help to communicate the message of the play?

The Monkey's Paw

by W. W. Jacobs

Dramatized by Harriet Dexter

SETTING

Scene 1

Time: About 1870

Setting: *The living room of the Whites' modest cottage, in a rural area of England. Two or three easy chairs are near the fireplace at right. A rocking chair with knitting basket beside it is nearby. A table holding a tea service is near the easy chairs. A coat rack with a few wraps, including the Sergeant-Major's raincoat and hat, is up left center, with umbrellas in an umbrella stand beside it. Door to kitchen is down right, door to outside is down left. A curtained window is in left wall, and a few stairs up left lead to the upstairs.*

At rise: **Mr. White** *and* **Sergeant-Major Morris** *sit near the fireplace.* **Morris** *holds a teacup which he fills from time to time.* **Herbert** *stands near* **Mrs. White**, *who is in rocking chair, knitting. Rain is heard throughout the entire scene.*

Mr. White.   (*admiringly*) You certainly brought a fund of interesting tales home from India, Morris.

Mrs. White.   I should think you'd find it rather dull back in England.

Morris.   No, Mrs. White, I'm happy to be retired. Thirty years in the army is a long time. Always an honor to serve Her Majesty, of course, but nothing compares with one's native land.

Mr. White.   We're fortunate that you took the cottage down the road. (*smiles at* **Mrs. White**) My wife has been fretting about the loneliness.

Mrs. White.   (*frowning*) We're so out of the way here. Seems as if we've been forgotten by the authorities. (*nods toward outside*) When it rains like this, the pathway's a bog, and the road's a torrent.

Herbert.   (*laughing*) You'll make the Sergeant-Major sorry he ever returned, Mother.

Morris.   No danger of that. I'm enjoying the peace and quiet.

Herbert.   You certainly didn't lack excitement in India. (*wistfully*) Sometimes I wonder if I'll be making farm machinery for the rest of my life.

Morris.   Stick to your job at the factory, Herbert. Better off in the long run.

Mr. White.   I know how Herbert feels. I'd like to visit India myself. I've heard so much about those temples . . . and the jugglers and snakecharmers.

Herbert.   (*eagerly*) Didn't you mention a rather remarkable monkey's paw, or something of the sort last week,

Sergeant-Major? (**Mr. and Mrs. White** *lean forward with anticipation.*)

Morris. *(uncomfortably)* It was nothing. At least, nothing worth hearing.

Mr. White. *(grinning)* You can't stop now, Morris.

Morris. *(offhandedly)* Oh, it's just what you might call a bit of magic. (**Whites** *watch with rapt attention as he fumbles in his pocket.*) Nothing but an ordinary little paw dried to a mummy. *(takes a black, shrivelled object from pocket)*

Mrs. White. *(recoiling[1])* Ugh—nasty!

Herbert. *(taking paw and examining it)* It really is a monkey's paw! *(hands it to* **Mr. White***)*

Mr. White. What's so special about it?

Morris. A very old fakir—a holy man—put a spell on it. He wanted to show that fate rules people's lives and those who interfere with fate do so to their sorrow.

Mr. White. What is the spell?

Morris. Three different men may have three wishes on the paw. (**Mrs. White** *laughs nervously.*)

Herbert. *(grinning with disbelief)* Did you have three, sir?

Morris. *(somberly)* I did.

Mrs. White. And were they granted?

Morris. They were. The man who owned the paw before me had his three wishes. I don't know what the first two were, but his wife told me *(pauses impressively)* the third was for death. (**Mrs. White** *gasps.* **Mr. White** *goes to her, smiling reassuringly.*)

Herbert. If you've already had your three, sir, the paw is no good to you, so why do you keep it?

Morris. *(shrugging)* I thought of selling it, but it has caused enough mischief already. Besides, I don't think people

---

[1] shrinking away in fear and disgust

would buy it. Many think it's a fairy tale, and the others
want to try it first and pay me afterward.

Mr. White.   If you could have another three wishes, would
you?

Morris.   No. (*He suddenly takes the paw from* **Mr. White** *and
throws it into the fire. The others are startled.*)

Mr. White.   (*grabbing paw from the fire*) Why did you do that?

Morris.   Better let it burn!

Mr. White.   If you don't want it, Morris, give it to me.

Morris.   You can keep it, but don't blame me for what happens!

Mrs. White.   (*shuddering*) I don't like it, dear.

Herbert.   I say let's keep it. What harm can come, whether
it's a fairy tale or not?

Mr. White.   (*staring at the paw, fascinated*) How do you make
the wish?

Morris.   (*sighing resignedly*) Hold it up in your right hand
and wish aloud. But I warn you of the consequences.

Mrs. White.   (*crossing to table*) I'm going to clear the dishes,
and if you're determined to make a wish, Father, you can
wish for two more pairs of arms for me! (**Herbert** *and* **Mrs.
White** *laugh as* **Mr. White** *holds paw up in his right hand.* **Morris**
leaps at him with a cry of alarm and knocks his arm down.)

Morris.   If you must wish, wish for something sensible!

Mr. White.   (*sheepishly*) I was just having a bit of fun, Morris.
I wouldn't wish for anything frivolous.[2]

Morris.   Best not to wish at all! The results can be disastrous. (*slowly*) And what happens seems so natural you
might attribute it to coincidence.

Mrs. White.   (*soothingly*) If it will ease your fears, Sergeant-
Major, I can't think of anything we'd wish for.

---

[2] silly

Morris.   But the temptation will remain as long as you own the paw. *(sighs)* I wish I'd kept quiet about it. *(He rises.)*

Herbert.   You're not going, are you, sir? It's still early.

Morris.   Better to start now before the storm worsens.

Herbert.   *(bringing* **Morris**'s *hat and coat)* I'll be happy to walk part of the way with you.

Mr. White.   *(quickly)* I'll do it, Herbert. I need some exercise, anyway. *(He ignores* **Morris**'s *protests and gets his coat and umbrella.)*

Mrs. White.   Goodnight, Sergeant-Major.

Herbert.   *(smiling)* Don't worry about the monkey's paw, sir. I think you'll find us safe and sound the next time you come.

Morris.   *(solemnly)* I hope so, Herbert. *(shaking hands)* Until next week, then. *(He follows* **Mr. White** *out.)*

Mrs. White.   *(returning to her dishes)* Such an interesting man. What do you make of that story about the monkey's paw, Herbert?

Herbert.   *(laughing)* I'd say there's as much truth to that as there is in the rest of his tales. The Sergeant-Major has a lively imagination. (**Mrs. White** *laughs and takes dishes to kitchen.* **Herbert** *goes to mantel, takes paw, and is idly examining it when* **Mr. White** *returns.)* Back already? (**Mr. White** *enters.)*

Mr. White.   *(evasively,*[3] *as he hangs up his coat)* Morris didn't want me to accompany him. He thinks I'm not as used to foul weather as he is.

Mrs. White.   *(eyeing him shrewdly)* The truth, Father. How much did you give him for the monkey's paw?

Mr. White.   *(guiltily)* A trifle. He didn't want it. Told me again to throw the thing away.

———————

[3]in a purposely vague way

Herbert.   *(laughing)* You're not likely to do that, after paying for it. *(with a sly glance at* **Mrs. White**) Better wish to be an emperor, Father. Then you won't be henpecked.

Mrs. White.   *(pretending to be shocked)* Better wish for a more respectful son! *(as* **Mr. White** *takes paw from mantel and looks at it thoughtfully)* What are you doing with that?

Mr. White.   Wondering what I should wish for. It seems to me I have all I want.

Mrs. White.   *(promptly)* Then it's best not to wish. You heard what the Sergeant-Major said. Why tempt fate?

Herbert.   Wouldn't you be happy if you could pay off the mortgage, Father? It would only take two hundred pounds.

Mr. White.   *(slowly)* Why, yes, Herbert. That would be a great help. *(He glances questioningly at* **Mrs. White**. *She shrugs, goes to her rocking chair and takes up her knitting. Hesitantly.)* Should I, Herbert?

Herbert.   Of course! You know you're keen on it, and you have nothing to lose. *(as his parents look at him sharply)* I think that's all bosh—about tempting fate.

Mr. White.   *(holding up paw and clearing his throat self-consciously)* I wish for two hundred pounds! *(Instantly he cries out and drops the paw.* **Herbert** *hurries to his side and* **Mrs. White** *rises in alarm.)*

Herbert.   What is it, Father?

Mrs. White.   Why did you do that?

Mr. White.   *(recoiling from the paw)* It twisted in my hands like a snake—just as I made the wish!

Mrs. White.   You must have fancied it.

Mr. White.   I didn't fancy it! Gave me quite a shock.

Herbert.   Well, I don't see the money. *(He picks up paw and puts it on mantel.)*

Mr. White.   You're not likely to see the money yet. Remember what Morris said! It'll come about in such an unexpected way, we'll put it down to coincidence.

Herbert. (*grinning*) Then I shan't stand about and wait. I have a job to go to in the morning, you know. (*starting toward stairs*) I expect you'll find the cash in a big bag on your bed, and a horrible goblin watching as you open it.

Mr. White. (*uneasily*) I wouldn't jest[4] about it, Herbert.

Mrs. White. Perhaps Herbert is right, Father. We should treat this whole episode as a prank. Anyhow, even if we did get the two hundred pounds, how could it hurt us?

Herbert. It could drop on Father's head from the sky. (*He laughs, kisses his mother, and exits upstairs.* **Mr. White** *is staring at the paw with a troubled expression.*)

Mrs. White. (*putting a hand on his arm*) Tomorrow will bring sunny skies, and all this turmoil about the monkey's paw will seem nothing but foolishness.

Mr. White. Perhaps.

Mrs. White. We'd best get to bed. (*She waits a moment, but* **Mr. White** *shows no inclination to leave. She shakes her head and exits upstairs.* **Mr. White** *slowly crosses to the mantel, as though against his will, picks up the paw and stares at it with growing repugnance.[5] Then he quickly replaces it on mantel and goes upstairs. Curtain.*)

SETTING

Scene 2

Time: The next afternoon.

Setting: *Same as Scene 1.*

At rise: The curtains are open and sunshine streams through the windows. **Mrs. White** *is dusting the furniture and* **Mr. White** *enters from kitchen.*

---

[4] joke around

[5] strong dislike or distaste

Mrs. White.   Finished your gardening?

Mr. White.   (*nodding*) Herbert will be happy to know the green beans are coming up nicely. He's so partial to them. (*smiles faintly*) Perhaps we should use the two hundred pounds for a really fine vegetable garden . . . one that will take care of itself.

Mrs. White.   (*laughing*) We won't see any two hundred pounds. I'm convinced that ugly little paw has no magic powers, and it doesn't look very sinister in the light of day.

Mr. White.   I'm not so sure of that.

Mrs. White.   Why, Herbert saw through that story at once. Remember his funny remarks?

Mr. White.   (*nodding*) I expect he'll have even funnier things to say about it when he gets home this evening. (*darkly*) But for all that, the thing did move in my hand. That I'll swear to.

Mrs. White.   (*mildly*) You thought it did.

Mr. White.   It did. There was no thought about it. I had just—(He stops as **Mrs. White** *suddenly looks toward the window.*) What's the matter?

Mrs. White.   I heard something. (*puts dustcloth into her pocket and crosses to window*) Yes. Someone is coming toward the gate. (*She peers out as* **Mr. White** *joins her.*) Do you know that man?

Mr. White.   (*looking*) I'm not likely to know anyone who wears a silk hat. Not that it matters. I think he's leaving.

Mrs. White.   (*perplexed*[6]) But he started to open the gate. He can't seem to make up his mind. (*Sound of gate clanging shut is heard offstage.*) Here he comes! (*She hurriedly takes off apron and puts it under the rocking chair cushion. She smoothes her hair as knock is heard at the door.* **Mr. White** *opens door to* **Caller**.)

---

[6]puzzled

Mr. White.   Good morning, sir. (*motions* **Caller** *in; sociably*) Not really morning anymore. I finished my gardening half an hour ago and it was just going on noon then. (*pauses uncertainly as* **Caller** *remains just inside door, twisting his hat in his hands*)

Mrs. White.   (*coming forward*) Is there something we can do for you, sir?

Caller.   I was asked to call. (*nervously*) I'm from Mark and Meggins. (**Mr.** *and* **Mrs. White** *look at one another apprehensively.*[7])

Mrs. White.   (*tremulously*[8]) Has something happened to Herbert? (*When* **Caller** *does not respond she panics.*) What is it?

Mr. White.   (*putting his arm around her*) There, Mother, don't jump to conclusions. (*to* **Caller**, *beseechingly*[9]) You've not brought bad news, have you?

Caller.   (*averting*[10] *his face*) I'm sorry.

Mrs. White.   Is he hurt? Tell us, is he hurt?

Caller.   (*softly*) Badly hurt. (*as* **Mrs. White** *cries out*) But he is not in any pain.

Mrs. White.   Oh, thank God for that! Thank God—(*She breaks off with a gasp as his meaning dawns on her, and turns blindly to her husband, who grasps her hand.*)

Caller.   It was an accident . . . with the machinery. (**Mr.** *and* **Mrs. White** *stare at him.*)

Mr. White.   (*tonelessly*) The machinery. (*after a pause*) He was the only one left to us. It is hard.

Caller.   (*going to window and looking out*) The firm wished me to convey their sincere sympathy to you. (*miserably*)

---

[7] fearfully; uneasily

[8] in a trembling, quivering way

[9] asking earnestly; in a begging manner

[10] turning away

I beg you to understand that I am only their servant, and merely obeying orders.

Mrs. White. (*dully*) Yes. Obeying orders.

Caller. I was to say that Mark and Meggins disclaims all responsibility. But in consideration of your son's services, they wish to present you with a certain sum as compensation. (**Mr.** *and* **Mrs. White** *stare at him in growing horror.*)

Mr. White. (*barely audible*) How much?

Caller. (*taking an envelope from his coat*) Two hundred pounds. (**Mrs. White** *screams and her husband catches her as she sways. Quick curtain.*)

Scene 3

Time: One week later. Night.

Setting: *The same.*

At rise: The stage is dimly lit. **Mrs. White**, *who is in her night-clothes, is huddled in a chair, sobbing. After a moment,* **Mr. White**, *in robe and slippers, and holding a candle or kerosene lamp, comes down the stairs. He pauses for a moment at foot of stairs, sadly regarding his wife, then places candle on table and goes to her.*

Mr. White. (*tenderly*) Come back to bed. You will be cold here.

Mrs. White. It is colder for my son! (*She sobs.*)

Mr. White. (*trying to coax her to get up*) He has been gone for a week. Your tears cannot bring him back.

Mrs. White. (*lashing out at him*) He was all we had! When we lost the other children I promised myself I would never let anything happen to Herbert! (*rises and pounds* *him with her fists)* Why did you make that wish? The wish that killed him!

Mr. White. *(catching her hands)* Do you think I have not asked myself that same question ever since his death? I will never know a peaceful moment until I am laid in the ground beside him!

Mrs. White. *(collapsing against him)* Forgive me. You are no more to blame than I am. I should have stopped you. The Sergeant-Major warned us. *(She cries bitterly.)*

Mr. White. Poor Morris. He is suffering almost as much as we are.

Mrs. White. I know he is. But I wish we had never met him! I wish we had never heard of the monkey's paw! *(She clings to him, weeping helplessly for a moment, then suddenly stiffens. She pulls away from her husband, her eyes blazing with excitement.)* The monkey's paw!

Mr. White. *(startled)* What? *(looking about frantically)* Where?

Mrs. White. Why didn't I think of it before? *(shaking him)* Get it! *(shouting)* Get it quickly! *(seeing his distracted expression)* You haven't destroyed it, have you?

Mr. White. No. I—I've hidden it. Why?

Mrs. White. *(ecstatically[11])* Don't you understand? We're saved! I just now thought of it!

Mr. White. *(frightened)* Thought of what?

Mrs. White. The other two wishes! We've only had one!

Mr. White. *(fiercely)* Was one not enough?

Mrs. White. No! We'll have one more! *(pushing him)* Get the monkey's paw and wish our boy alive again!

Mr. White. You are mad! Go back to bed—you don't know what you are saying!

Mrs. White. *(shouting)* Get it! Hurry!

Mr. White. *(shouting)* Didn't you hear what Morris said? We interfere with fate at our peril!

---

[11] in a very happy or delighted way

Mrs. White. *(raging at him)* We have already interfered with fate and lost our son! Now we shall have him back! Get the monkey's paw! *(She watches breathlessly as* **Mr. White** *stumbles to the umbrella stand, reaches in and pulls out the paw.)* Now—make the wish!

Mr. White. *(staring at paw, and whispering)* I don't want to see him. I'm afraid.

Mrs. White. What are you muttering about? Make the wish!

Mr. White. *(pleading)* Leave him in the grave, Mother. Let him rest.

Mrs. White. *(rushing at him)* Wish!

Mr. White. *(slowly, fearfully holding up the paw)* I wish my son alive again. *(His arm twitches violently, and he cries out as the paw flies out of his hand. He sinks, trembling, into a chair as* **Mrs. White** *runs to the window and parts the curtains. She stands at the window and stares out into the darkness, as though in a trance. After a moment,* **Mr. White** *joins her.)* Don't stay here. You must sleep. *(She pulls her hand away without looking at him.)* This cannot help us. It can only hurt us further. *(She does not respond and he shakes his head in defeat.)* Good night, then. *(He starts upstairs, and suddenly* **Mrs. White** *turns sharply.)*

Mrs. White. What was that? That creaking sound?

Mr. White. Nothing. A rat inside the walls. *(***Mrs. White** *turns back to window and a moment later a single knock is heard at the door.* **Mr. White** *freezes on the stairs, and* **Mrs. White** *turns to look at the door. The knock is repeated, louder. A third, imperative knock brings* **Mr. White** *down the stairs as* **Mrs. White** *rushes to the door.)*

Mrs. White. It's Herbert!

Mr. White. *(trying to hold her)* What are you going to do?

Mrs. White. *(struggling against him)* My boy is out there! Let me go!

Mr. White. You mustn't! It will destroy us!

Mrs. White. Let me go! I must open the door!

Mr. White. Whatever it is out there, don't let it in!

Mrs. White. (*blazing at him*) You're afraid of your own son! (As **Mr. White** *tries to pull her away from the door, she screams over her shoulder.*) I'm coming, Herbert! I'm coming! (*She finally breaks away and reaches the door, but she is unable to pull back the bolt. As she struggles with it,* **Mr. White** *begins searching the floor frantically for the paw.*) Help me! I can't open the door!

Mr. White. No! Leave it closed! (*A sudden, strong knock is heard, quickly followed by more. The knocking builds until it reaches a crescendo that reverberates through the room.* **Mrs. White** *manages to free the bolt and pull the door open. A howling rush of wind is heard.*)

Mrs. White. I'm here, Herbert! I'm here! (*She rushes out, just as* **Mr. White** *finds the paw. He scrambles to his feet, and at the same moment* **Mrs. White**'s *terrified scream is heard offstage. She screams again and stumbles into the house.* **Mr. White** *slams and bolts the door.*) No! No! (**Mr. White** *holds her.*) Don't let me see him again! His face— (*The knocking begins again. It becomes louder and louder, threatening to break down the door.* **Mr. White** *supports his wife with one arm, and with the other hand holds the monkey's paw high.*)

Mr. White. (*shouting over the din*) I wish my son back in his grave—at peace forever! (*The knocking ceases.* **Mrs. White** *collapses in chair, and* **Mr. White** *hurls the monkey's paw into the fireplace. He grimly strikes a match as the curtain closes.*)

THE END

REVIEWING AND INTERPRETING

Record your answers to these questions in your personal literature notebook. Follow the directions for each part.

REVIEWING   Try to complete each of these sentences without looking back at the play.

Recalling Facts   1. Sergeant-Major Morris had spent many years in the army in
a. China.
b. India.
c. Egypt.
d. Turkey.

Identifying Cause and Effect   2. Sergeant-Major Morris throws the monkey's paw into the fire because
a. he believes that it can cause only trouble.
b. it is so shriveled and ugly.
c. he wants to punish the White family.
d. the paw has moved in his hand.

Identifying Sequence   3. Just after Mrs. White suggests that her husband wish for two more arms for her, Morris
a. decides to go home.
b. throws the paw into the fire.
c. tells Mr. White how to make the wish properly.
d. warns Mr. White to wish for something sensible.

Understanding Main Ideas   4. The Whites decide to make a wish for money because
a. Morris urges them to.
b. they really need it and can't find any other way to raise it.
c. they think there's nothing to lose, and they could use the money.
d. they want to prove to Morris that superstitions are true.

Recognizing Literary Elements (Climax)

5. The climax, or turning point, of the play occurs when
   a. Mrs. White demands that Mr. White wish Herbert alive again.
   b. Mr. White wishes that his son were back in his grave.
   c. The Caller tells the Whites that their son has died.
   d. Mr. White throws the paw in the fireplace and lights a match.

INTERPRETING To complete these sentences, you may look back at the play if you'd like.

Making Inferences

6. When the Caller arrives, he looks like he can't make up his mind whether or not to open the gate. He probably hesitates because he is feeling
   a. too important to go to this small cottage.
   b. overtired after his long walk from town.
   c. nervous about delivering such bad news.
   d. confused about whether this is the right house.

Analyzing

7. The Whites are absolutely convinced that the wish on the monkey's paw has caused Herbert's death when
   a. they make a second wish.
   b. Mr. White insists that the paw moved when he made the wish.
   c. the Caller explains that Herbert died in an accident with the machinery.
   d. the Caller presents them with exactly two hundred pounds.

Predicting Outcomes

8. When the Whites hear another amazing story from Morris, they probably will
   a. believe it.
   b. not believe it.
   c. not listen.
   d. start to laugh.

Making
Generalizations

9. Mr. and Mrs. White would *not* agree with the statement that
  a. you should be careful what you wish for.
  b. getting three wishes will make you happy for life.
  c. you should be happy with what you have today.
  d. people are worth more than any amount of money.

Understanding
Literary Elements
(Character)

10. Which character is convinced that the monkey's paw is worthless?
  a. Herbert
  b. Mr. White
  c. the Caller
  d. Mrs. White

Now check your answers with your teacher. Study the questions you answered incorrectly. What types of questions were they? Talk with your teacher about ways to work on those skills.

Setting

One of the most important elements of a play is its setting. The *setting* is the time and place in which events take place. By describing and developing the setting, the playwright puts audiences in the right frame of mind to anticipate upcoming events. For example, when the curtain rises and an audience sees the inside of a log cabin and people dressed in eighteenth-century clothing, they get ready to see a historical play.

Every play, movie, or television show that you see has a setting. Sometimes the settings are very detailed. Consider the setting of your favorite family comedy on TV. After seeing the living room where the story is set, you might feel as if you know the house well. The setting is so realistic that you probably could predict what the other rooms of the house look like even if they are never shown.

At other times, however, the settings are very simple. In some stage plays, you may see nearly empty stages with only a few stools or ladders for actors to sit or stand on. Again, even these basic settings are important. Even though they are not elaborate in their detail, they still get you ready for the play. Simple settings are flexible. They can stand for anything that playwrights and directors decide they should be. They suggest that in order to enjoy the play, you must be flexible and imaginative too.

One of the ways in which the setting of a play prepares you for what is coming is by creating a mood. If the curtain rises on a dark moor with lightning flashing and thunder rumbling, you are likely to feel uneasy and maybe even a bit frightened.

The setting also determines what characters are likely to be featured in the play, as well as what events are likely to happen. The stormy moor will probably not feature a group of tennis players looking for just the right court for a game. Instead, the characters and action will match the frightening setting.

In these lessons, you will look at the ways in which author W. W. Jacobs and playwright Harriet Dexter use the setting to tell the story of *The Monkey's Paw*:

1. They use the setting to create a mood.

2. They use the setting to reveal and develop the characters in the play.

3. They use the setting to communicate the theme of the play.

LESSON 1 | SETTING AND MOOD

When playwrights create settings, they are aware that they are also creating moods. The audience's feelings are affected by what they see and hear on stage. That's why playwrights think about the setting carefully before describing it in the stage directions. They want just the right background for the characters to act out the play.

Read the following description of the setting at the beginning of *The Monkey's Paw*. How would you describe the mood that the stage direction is trying to create?

Setting: *The living room of the Whites' modest cottage, in a rural area of England. Two or three easy chairs are near the fireplace at right. A rocking chair with knitting basket beside it is nearby. A table holding a tea service is near the easy chairs. A coat rack with a few wraps, including the Sergeant-Major's raincoat and hat, is up left center, with umbrellas in an umbrella stand beside it. Door to kitchen is down right, door to outside is down left. A curtained window is in left wall, and a few stairs up left lead to the upstairs.*

The room in which the play opens is warm and cozy. The furnishings are described as "easy chairs near the fireplace" and a "rocking chair with knitting basket beside it." Both of these images create feelings of comfort and security. The stage directions also mention familiar, homey objects such as a coat rack, a raincoat and hat, and umbrellas. They tell us that it is raining outside, but inside the house it is warm and dry. The tea service gives us a hint that the play takes place in England many years ago, where polite people served tea at an afternoon break time. The curtains on the window suggest that the house is well cared for and loved as a family home.

Playwright Harriet Dexter not only describes the scenery and props that the audience will see at the beginning of the play. She also tells readers who will be in the scene and what they will be doing as the play begins.

> *At rise:* **Mr. White** *and* **Sergeant-Major Morris** *sit near the fireplace.* **Morris** *holds a teacup which he fills from time to time.* **Herbert** *stands near* **Mrs. White**, *who is in rocking chair, knitting. Rain is heard throughout the entire scene.*

The phrase *at rise* refers to what the audience sees when the curtain rises. In the scene described above, the audience sees a pleasant scene of two men drinking tea as they sit in easy chairs near the fireplace. They also see a young man standing near an older woman who is quietly knitting. The actors and their actions work together with the setting to set a peaceful mood at the beginning of the play.

EXERCISE 1

Read this set of stage directions. Then use what you have learned in this lesson to answer the questions that follow.

Setting: *The same.*
At rise: *The stage is dimly lit.* **Mrs. White,** *who is in her nightclothes, is huddled in a chair, sobbing. After a moment,* **Mr. White,** *in robe and slippers, and holding a candle or kerosene lamp, comes down the stairs. He pauses for a moment at foot of stairs, sadly regarding his wife, then places candle on table and goes to her.*

1. The playwright has told you that the setting is the same— that is, the scene takes place in the same room as the previous scenes. It is true that most items are the same, but the scene's mood is different from the mood of the first scene. How would you describe the mood of this setting? How does the lowered lighting affect the mood?

2. Before a word is spoken, you know that the mood has changed. The characters are dressed differently now. Their actions convey that their moods have changed as well. How do their clothes and their silent actions affect the mood?

Now check your answers with your teacher. Review this part of the lesson if you don't understand why an answer was incorrect.

 WRITING ON YOUR OWN 1

Use what you have learned in this lesson to complete the following activity:

- Choose one of the following moods. Then picture a setting that you could use to create that mood:

  peace   anger   excitement   fear   happiness

- What objects or scenery would help to create the mood? List some words or phrases that you could use to describe what you would see, feel, and hear. For example, if you want to create a peaceful mood, you might picture a bedroom in a beautiful country home. Phrases you could use to describe the room might include "a warm, crackling fire in the fireplace," "a feather bed with an old-fashioned quilt," and a "kitten asleep on the windowsill."

• Use the words and phrases you just listed to write a paragraph describing your setting. Remember that everything in your description should help convey the mood.

• Reread your finished description. Were you successful in creating the mood? Make any changes that would improve the paragraph. Then store it in your writing portfolio.

LESSON 2 | SETTING AND CHARACTERS

You know that the setting sets the mood and prepares audiences for the action of a play. It also prepares audiences for the kinds of characters they will see. What kinds of characters would you expect to see, for example, if the curtain rose on the bridge of a high-tech spaceship? You probably would be ready to see crew members in futuristic uniforms or perhaps even alien life forms. But you wouldn't expect to see a farmer in overalls. A farmer simply wouldn't work in this setting.

Playwrights carefully create settings that will coordinate with the characters they want to write about. Playwrights also make sure that the settings help to explain a little about the characters. Read these lines from *The Monkey's Paw*. They reveal Mr. and Mrs. White as good-natured people who are happy to be living a quiet life in the country.

Mrs. White. (*crossing to table*) I'm going to clear the dishes, and if you're determined to make a wish, Father, you can wish for two more pairs of arms for me! (**Herbert** *and* **Mrs. White** *laugh as* **Mr. White** *holds paw up in his right hand.* **Morris** *leaps at him with a cry of alarm and knocks his arm down.*)

Morris. If you must wish, wish for something sensible!

Mr. White. (*sheepishly*) I was just having a bit of fun, Morris. I wouldn't wish for anything frivolous.

Morris. Best not to wish at all! The results can be disastrous. (*slowly*) And what happens seems so natural you might attribute it to coincidence.

Mrs. White. (*soothingly*) If it will ease your fears, Sergeant-Major, I can't think of anything we'd wish for.

EXERCISE 2

Read the following passage, which further describes the Whites' life in the country. Then use what you have learned in this lesson to answer the questions.

Mr. White. We're fortunate that you took the cottage down the road. (*smiles at* **Mrs. White**) My wife has been fretting about the loneliness.

Mrs. White. (*frowning*) We're so out of the way here. Seems as if we've been forgotten by the authorities. (*nods toward outside*) When it rains like this, the pathway's a bog, and the road's a torrent.

1. How does the setting affect the Whites' attitude toward Morris's stories? Why does it make them more likely to welcome his tales about India?

2. The Whites don't seem to get many visitors. How does their isolation affect their desire for excitement? Do you think it makes them more or less likely to try out the monkey's paw?

Now check your answers with your teacher. Review this part of the lesson if you don't understand why an answer was incorrect.

 WRITING ON YOUR OWN [2]

In this exercise you will use what you have learned in the lesson to describe characters you might find in particular settings.

- Choose one of the following settings and picture the characters you would be likely to find there.

  a busy downtown street
  a country general store
  a safari on the plains of Africa
  a city bus filled with people

- Focus on three characters who could appear in your chosen setting. Divide a sheet of paper into three columns. List any words or phrases that could be used to describe the way the characters look, act, and sound. Tell about what they are wearing. Don't try to describe their feelings or thoughts. Just concentrate on what can be seen or heard.
- Write a short description of each character. Use the words and phrases you just listed.

LESSON 3   SETTING AND THEME

If you were a writer who wanted to share an idea or a belief with readers, you could write an essay, clearly stating your opinion and backing it up with reasons and arguments. Or you could write a speech that would persuade people to agree with you. Some writers choose these ways of sharing a message, or theme. Others use short stories, novels, and plays to do the job.

One of the themes of *The Monkey's Paw* is that we don't realize how wonderful everyday life is until it is taken away. We wish for some event that we think will make life better, and we don't appreciate what we have until it's too late.

Read the following passage. Notice how the setting emphasizes Mr. and Mrs. White's happiness with the simple pleasures of life.

Scene 2
Time: *The next afternoon.*
Setting: *Same as Scene 1.*
At rise: The curtains are open and sunshine streams through the windows. **Mrs. White** *is dusting the furniture and* **Mr. White** *enters from kitchen.*

Mrs. White.   Finished your gardening?

Mr. White.   (*nodding*) Herbert will be happy to know the green beans are coming up nicely. He's so partial to them. (*smiles faintly*) Perhaps we should use the two hundred pounds for a really fine vegetable garden . . . one that will take care of itself.

Mrs. White.   (*laughing*) We won't see any two hundred pounds. I'm convinced that ugly little paw has no magic powers, and it doesn't look very sinister in the light of day.

Mr. White.   I'm not so sure of that.

Mrs. White.   Why, Herbert saw through that story at once. Remember his funny remarks?

Mrs. White.   (*nodding*) I expect he'll have even funnier things to say about it when he gets home this evening.

Mr. White gets pleasure out of tending his vegetable garden and looks forward to sharing his produce with his son. Mrs. White enjoys her son's sense of humor and his intelligence. The couple seem to have all they want from life.

EXERCISE [3]

Read this stage direction. Then use what you have learned about setting to answer the questions that follow.

> *At rise: The stage is dimly lit.* **Mrs. White**, *who is in her nightclothes, is huddled in a chair, sobbing. After a moment,* **Mr. White**, *in robe and slippers, and holding a candle or kerosene lamp, comes down the stairs. He pauses for a moment at foot of stairs, sadly regarding his wife, then places candle on table and goes to her.*

1. The setting is now dark and sad. The actions of the Whites have caused the change. What themes about money or curiosity does the changed setting suggest?

2. Although the setting has changed, Mr. White continues to treat his wife with kindness. What theme might his actions suggest?

Now check your answers with your teacher. Review this part of the lesson if you don't understand why an answer was incorrect.

WRITING ON YOUR OWN [3]

In this exercise you will use what you have learned to write a summary of a story that conveys a particular theme. Follow these steps:

• Read this list of sayings, and then choose one to write a story about.

The best things in life are free.
You can't tell a book by its cover.
No news is good news.

- Review the settings you listed in Writing on Your Own 2. Choose one of those settings, or if you'd like, think of a setting of your own.
- Write the saying you chose at the top of a sheet of paper. Then write a brief summary of an original story that conveys your chosen theme and takes place in your chosen setting. Describe the characters briefly. The characters and actions should be logical, given your particular theme and setting. Your story needs only a few events. Just be sure the story's message is clear.

DISCUSSION GUIDES

1. Have you read or heard any other stories in which the characters make three wishes? Work with a group to list stories that feature three wishes. For each story, fill out a form like the one below. Along with the title of the story, list the characters and the three wishes. Tell what happened to the characters as a result of their wishes. Then share your information with the rest of the class. Decide whether most characters enjoyed or regretted the results of their wishes.

> Title of Story:
> Characters:
> First Wish:
> Second Wish:
> Third Wish:
> Result or Results:

2. If you had three wishes, what would you wish for? With your classmates, list as many wishes as you can on the board. After you have listed about 30 wishes, categorize them in some way. For example, how many are personal wishes? How many are wishes for the entire world? How many are family-related? How many are related to community life? Based on your class's list, what conclusions can you draw about people's wishes and desires?

3. How much do you know about England's relationship with India? With a partner, do some research about England's role in India's history. Why were Morris and other British soldiers stationed in India? How and when did the relationship between the countries change? What is England's relationship to India today? Write a short report on the topic and present it to the rest of the class.

CREATE A SETTING

In this unit you have seen how the author and playwright of *The Monkey's Paw* have created a setting that helps tell the play's story. In this exercise, you will use stage directions for a play to write about a setting with a particular mood.

If you have questions about the writing process, refer to Using the Writing Process (page 261).

- Review the writing assignments that you completed in this unit, including: 1) details about a place, 2) a paragraph about a setting that conveys a mood, 3) descriptions of three characters from a chosen setting, and 4) a summary of story events that express a theme in a particular setting.
- Study the format of the stage directions at the beginning of *The Monkey's Paw.* Follow the same format in this exercise. First, identify the time your play is set in. Label this section *Time.* Here is an example:
    Time: About 1950. Sunrise.
- Rewrite the description of the setting that you created for Writing on Your Own 1. Describe the props you want on the stage at the beginning of the play. Point out where each item should be. Remember to include scenery and objects that will help create your chosen mood. Label this section *Setting.*
- Next, describe the characters who will be on stage when the curtain rises. Tell what the characters will be doing and make sure their positions and actions all help to develop the mood. Label this section *At rise.* Include any special lighting or sounds that would help to create the mood.
- Ask a classmate to read your first draft and identify the mood of the setting. If your reader can't figure out the mood you are hoping to create add helpful details or remove confusing ones.
- Proofread your setting for spelling, grammar, punctuation, capitalization, and formatting errors. Make a final copy and save it in your writing portfolio.

Theme

UNIT 6

Let Me Hear You Whisper

by Paul Zindel

INTRODUCTION

ABOUT THE SELECTION

Helen is an elderly woman who lives alone and enjoys caring for stray cats and dogs. She gets a job as a cleaning lady in a laboratory that performs scientific experiments on animals—particularly dolphins. At first Helen tries to obey her supervisor and ignore the dolphin that is kept in the lab, one of the rooms she cleans. Soon, however, she finds that she can no longer stand by without becoming involved in the fate of the friendly mammal.

ABOUT THE AUTHOR

Paul Zindel was born in 1936 in Staten Island, New York. When he was just 25 years old, he wrote his award-winning play *The Effect of Gamma Rays on Man-in-the-Moon Marigolds*. Years later, when the play was finally brought to the stage, it was named Best American play of the 1969–70 season by the New York Drama Critics Circle and won the Pulitzer Prize for Drama in 1971. In addition to his plays, Mr. Zindel has written numerous novels for young adults, including *The Pigman; I Never Loved Your Mind; My*

Darling, My Hamburger; A Begonia for Miss Applebaum; and *The Doom Stone*. Two of the themes he has explored in his writing are the emotional hurdles young people go through on their way to maturity and the interdependence of humans and animals.

ABOUT THE LESSONS

The lessons that follow *Let Me Hear You Whisper* focus on theme. The theme of a story or play is the message that the writer wants to share with his or her readers. Sometimes the theme is an important idea or lesson to be learned about life. At other times, the theme is a recurring question or issue that the author wants readers to think about. In a longer work, there is usually one main theme and several minor themes.

WRITING: DEVELOPING A THEME

At the end of this unit you will write a dialogue that develops a theme. The speakers whom you create will help you convey a message that you personally believe in. The suggestions below will help you get started:

- Think about some lessons you have learned from life. What values has your family taught you? What have you learned from your friends? What ideas about life have you learned at school or in your community?
- Fill in a chart like the one on the following page. In the right-hand column, list at least one lesson that you have learned from each group in the left-hand column.

People	Lessons
Your family	
Your friends	
Your school	
Your community	

- Save your chart. You will refer to it for ideas when you write your dialogue at the end of this unit.

AS YOU READ

Think about the following questions as you read. They will help you pay attention to the themes, or messages, presented in this play.

- What lessons or life values do the conflicts in this play bring to mind?
- How do the characters help to express the play's themes?
- How do your feelings about animals affect your understanding of the themes of the play?

Let Me Hear You Whisper

by Paul Zindel

Helen, *a little old cleaning lady who lives alone in a one-room apartment and spends most of her spare time feeding stray cats and dogs. She has just been hired to scrub floors in a laboratory that performs rather strange experiments with dolphins.*

Miss Moray, *a briskly efficient custodial supervisor who has to break* **Helen** *in to her new duties at the laboratory. She has a face that is so uptight she looks like she either throws stones at pigeons or teaches Latin.*

Dr. Crocus, *the dedicated man of science who devises and presides over the weird experiments.*

Mr. Fridge, *assistant to* **Dr. Crocus**. *He is so loyal and uncreative that if* **Dr. Crocus** *told him to stick his head in the mouth of a shark, he'd do it.*

Dan, *a talky janitor, also under* **Miss Moray**'s *control, who at every chance ducks out of the Manhattan laboratory for a beer at the corner bar.*

A Dolphin, *the subject of an experiment being performed by* **Dr. Crocus**.

Setting: *The action takes place in the hallway, laboratory, and specimen[1] room of a biology experimentation association located in Manhattan near the Hudson River.*

Time: *The action begins with the night shift on a Monday and ends the following Friday.*

ACT I/ Scene 1

(**Dr. Crocus** *and* **Mr. Fridge** *are leaving the laboratory where they have completed their latest experimental tinkering with a dolphin, and they head down a corridor to the elevator. The elevator door opens and* **Miss Moray** *emerges with* **Helen.**)

Miss Moray.   Dr. Crocus. Mr. Fridge. I'm so glad we've run into you. I want you to meet Helen.

Helen.   Hello. (**Dr. Crocus** *and* **Mr. Fridge** *nod and get on elevator.*)

Miss Moray.   Helen is the newest member of our Custodial Engineering Team. (**Miss Moray** *and* **Helen** *start down the hall.*)

Miss Moray.   Dr. Crocus is the guiding heart here at the American Biological Association Development for the Advancement of Brain Analysis. For short, we call it "Abadaba."

Helen.   I guess you have to. (*They stop at a metal locker at the end of the hall.*)

Miss Moray.   This will be your locker and your key. Your equipment is in this closet.

Helen.   I have to bring in my own hangers, I suppose.

---

[1] sample to be studied and analyzed

Miss Moray.   Didn't you find Personnel pleasant?

Helen.   They asked a lot of crazy questions.

Miss Moray.   Oh, I'm sorry. (*pause*) For instance.

Helen.   They wanted to know what went on in my head when I'm watching television in my living room and the audience laughs. They asked if I ever thought the audience was laughing at *me*.

Miss Moray.   (*laughing*) My, oh, my! (*pause*) What did you tell them?

Helen.   I don't have a TV.

Miss Moray.   I'm sorry.

Helen.   I'm not.

Miss Moray.   Yes. Now, it's really quite simple. That's our special soap solution. One tablespoon to a gallon of hot water, if I may suggest. (**Helen** *is busy running water into a pail which fits into a metal stand on wheels.*)

Miss Moray.   I'll start you in the laboratory. We like it done first. The specimen room next, and finally the hallway. By that time we'll be well toward morning, and if there are a few minutes left, you can polish the brass strip. (*She points to brass strip which runs around the corridor, halfway between ceiling and floor.*) Ready? Fine. (*They start down the hall,* **Miss Moray** *thumbing through papers on a clipboard.*)

Miss Moray.   You were with one concern for fourteen years, weren't you? Fourteen years with the Metal Climax Building. That's next to the Radio City Music Hall, isn't it, dear?

Helen.   Uh-huh.

Miss Moray.   They sent a marvelous letter of recommendation. My! Fourteen years on the seventeenth floor. You must be very proud. Why did you leave?

Helen.   They put in a rug. (**Miss Moray** *leads* **Helen** *into the laboratory, where* **Dan** *is picking up.*)

Miss Moray.   Dan, Helen will be taking Marguerita's place. Dan is the night porter for the fifth through ninth floors.

Dan.   Hiya!

Helen.   Hello. *(She looks around.)*

Miss Moray.   There's a crock on nine you missed, and the technicians on that floor have complained about the odor. (**Helen** *notices what appears to be a large tank of water with a curtain concealing its contents.)*

Helen.   What's that?

Miss Moray.   What? Oh, that's a dolphin, dear. But don't worry about anything except the floor. Dr. Crocus prefers us not to touch either the equipment or the animals.

Helen.   Do you keep him cramped up in that all the time?

Miss Moray.   We have a natatorium for it to exercise in, at Dr. Crocus's discretion.

Helen.   He really looks cramped. (**Miss Moray** *closes a curtain which hides the tank.)*

Miss Moray.   Well, you must be anxious to begin. I'll make myself available at the reception desk in the hall for a few nights in case any questions arise. Coffee break at two and six A.M. Lunch at four A.M. All clear?

Helen.   I don't need a coffee break.

Miss Moray.   Helen, we all need Perk-You-Ups. All of us.

Helen.   I don't want one.

Miss Moray.   They're compulsory.[2] *(pause)* Oh, Helen, I know you're going to fit right in with our little family. You're such a *nice* person. *(She exits.)* (**Helen** *immediately gets to work, moving her equipment into place and getting down on her hands and knees to scrub the floor.* **Dan** *exits.*

---

[2] required

Helen *gets in a few more rubs, glances at the silhouette of the dolphin's tank behind the curtain, and then continues. After a pause, a record begins to play.)*

Record.   "Let me call you sweetheart,

I'm in love with you.

Let me hear you whisper

That you love me, too."

*(**Helen**'s curiosity makes her open the curtain and look at the dolphin. He looks right back at her. She returns to her work, singing "Let Me Call You Sweetheart" to herself, missing a word here and there; but her eyes return to the dolphin. She becomes uncomfortable under his stare and tries to ease her discomfort by playing peek-a-boo with him. There is no response and she resumes scrubbing and humming. The dolphin then lets out a bubble or two and moves in the tank to bring his blowhole to the surface.)*

Dolphin.   Youuuuuuuuuuuu. *(**Helen** hears the sound, assumes she is mistaken, and goes on with her work.)*

Dolphin.   Youuuuuuuuuuuu. *(**Helen** has heard the sound more clearly this time. She is puzzled, contemplates a moment, and then decides to get up off the floor. She closes the curtain on the dolphin's tank and leaves the laboratory. She walks the length of the hall to **Miss Moray**, who is sitting at a reception desk near the elevator.)*

Miss Moray.   What is it, Helen?

Helen.   The fish is making some kinda funny noise.

Miss Moray.   Mammal, Helen. It's a mammal.

Helen.   The mammal's making some kinda funny noise.

Miss Moray.   Mammals are supposed to make funny noises.

Helen.   Yes, Miss Moray. *(**Helen** goes back to the lab. She continues scrubbing.)*

Dolphin.   Youuuuuuuuuuuu. *(She apprehensively approaches the* *curtain and opens it. Just then* **Dan** *barges in. He goes to get his reaching pole, and* **Helen** *hurriedly returns to scrubbing the floor.)*

Dan.   Bulb out on seven.

Helen.   What do they have that thing for?

Dan.   What thing?

Helen.   That.

Dan.   Yeah, he's something, ain't he? *(pause)* They're tryin' to get it to talk.

Helen.   Talk?

Dan.   Uh-huh, but he don't say nothing. They had one last year that used to laugh. It'd go "heh heh heh heh heh heh heh." Then they got another one that used to say, "Yeah, it's four o'clock." Everybody took pictures of that one. All the magazines and newspapers.

Helen.   It just kept saying "Yeah, it's four o'clock"?

Dan.   Until it died of pneumonia. They talk outta their blowholes, when they can talk, that is. Did you see the blowhole?

Helen.   No.

Dan.   Come on and take a look.

Helen.   I don't want to look at any blowhole.

Dan.   Miss Moray's at the desk. She won't see anything. (**Helen** *and* **Dan** *go to the tank. Their backs are to the lab door and they don't see Miss Moray open the door and watch them.)*

Dan.   This one don't say anything at all. They been playing that record every seven minutes for months, and it can't even learn a single word. Don't even say "Polly want a cracker."

Miss Moray.   Helen? (**Helen** *and* **Dan** *turn around.)*

Miss Moray.   Helen, would you mind stepping outside a moment?

Helen. Yes, Miss Moray.

Dan. I was just showing her something.

Miss Moray. Hadn't we better get on with our duties?

Dan. All right, Miss Moray. (**Miss Moray** *guides* **Helen** *out into the hall, and puts her arm around her as though taking her into her confidence.*)

Miss Moray. Helen, I called you out here because . . . well, frankly, I need your help.

Helen. He was just showing me . . .

Miss Moray. Dan is an idle-chatter breeder. How many times we've told him, "Dan, this is a scientific atmosphere you're employed in and we would appreciate a minimum of subjective communication." So—if you can help, Helen—and I'm sure you can, enormously—we'd be so grateful.

Helen. Yes, Miss Moray. (**Miss Moray** *leads* **Helen** *back to the lab.*)

Miss Moray. Now, we'll just move directly into the specimen room. The working conditions will be ideal for you in here. (**Helen** *looks ready to gag as she looks around the specimen room. It is packed with specimen jars of all sizes. Various animals and parts of animals are visible in their formaldehyde[3] baths.*)

Miss Moray. Now, you will be responsible not only for the floor area but the jars as well. A feather duster—here— is marvelous. (**Miss Moray** *smiles and exits. The sound of music and voice from beyond the walls floats over.*)

Record. "Let me call you sweetheart . . ." (**Helen** *gasps as her eyes fall upon one particular jar in which is floating a preserved human brain. The lights go down, ending* **Act I, Scene 1.**)

---

[3] liquid used to preserve the tissues and organs of humans and animals

ACT I/Scene 2

*(It is the next evening. **Helen** pushes her equipment into the lab. She opens the curtain so she can watch the dolphin as she works. She and the dolphin stare at each other.)*

Helen.   Youuuuuuuuuuuu. *(She pauses, watches for a response.)* Youuuuuuuuuuuu. *(Still no response. She turns her attention to her scrubbing for a moment.)* Polly want a cracker? Polly want a cracker? *(She wrings out a rag and resumes work.)* Yeah, it's four o'clock. Yeah, it's four o'clock. Polly want a cracker at four o'clock? *(She laughs at her own joke, then goes to the dolphin's tank and notices how sad he looks. She reaches her hand in and just touches the top of his head. He squirms and likes it.)*

Helen.   Heh heh heh heh heh heh heh heh heh. (**Miss Moray** *gets off the elevator and hears the peculiar sounds coming from the laboratory. She puts her head against the door.)*

Helen.   Heh heh heh heh heh . . .

Miss Moray.   *(entering)* Look how nicely the floor's coming along! You must have a special rinsing technique.

Helen.   Just a little vinegar in the rinse water.

Miss Moray.   You brought the vinegar yourself, just so the floors . . . they are sparkling, Helen. Sparkling! *(She pauses—looks at the dolphin, then at **Helen**.)* It's marvelous, Helen, how well you've adjusted.

Helen.   Thank you, Miss Moray.

Miss Moray.   Helen, the animals here are used for experimentation, and. . . . Well, take Marguerita. She had fallen in love with the mice. All three hundred of them. She seemed shocked when she found out Dr. Crocus was. . . using . . . them at the rate of twenty or so a day in connection with electrode implanting. She noticed them missing after a while and when I told her they'd been decapitated, she seemed terribly upset.

Helen.   What do they want with the fish—mammal?

Miss Moray.   Well, dolphins may have an intelligence equal to our own. And if we can teach them our language—or learn theirs—we'll be able to communicate.

Helen.   I can't understand you.

Miss Moray.   *(louder)* Communicate! Wouldn't it be wonderful?

Helen.   Oh, yeah. . . . They chopped the heads off three hundred mice? That's horrible.

Miss Moray.   You're so sensitive, Helen. Every laboratory in the country is doing this type of work. It's quite accepted.

Helen.   Every laboratory cutting off mouse heads!

Miss Moray.   Virtually . . .

Helen.   How many laboratories are there?

Miss Moray.   I don't know. I suppose at least five thousand.

Helen.   Five thousand times three hundred . . . that's a lot of mouse heads. Can't you just have one lab chop off a couple and then spread the word?

Miss Moray.   Now, Helen—this is exactly what I mean. You will do best not to become fond of the subject animals. When you're here a little longer you'll learn . . . well . . . there are some things you just have to accept on faith. (**Miss Moray** *exits, leaving the lab door open for* **Helen** *to move her equipment out.*)

Dolphin.   Whisper . . . (**Helen** pauses a moment.) Whisper to me. (*She exits as the lights go down, ending the scene.*)

ACT I/Scene 3

(*It is the next evening.* **Helen** *goes from her locker to the laboratory.*)

Dolphin.   Hear . . .

Helen.   What?

Dolphin. Hear me . . . (**Dan** *barges in with his hamper, almost frightening* **Helen** *to death. He goes to dolphin's tank.*)

Dan. Hiya, fella! How are ya? That reminds me. Gotta get some formaldehyde jars set up by Friday. If you want anything just whistle. (*He exits.* **Helen** *goes to the tank and reaches her hand out to pet the dolphin.*)

Helen. Hear. (*pause*) Hear.

Dolphin. Hear.

Helen. Hear me.

Dolphin. Hear me.

Helen. That's a good boy.

Dolphin. Hear me . . .

Helen. Oh, What a pretty fellow. Such a pretty fellow. (**Miss Moray** *enters.*)

Miss Moray. What are you doing, Helen?

Helen. I . . . Uh . . .

Miss Moray. Never mind. Go on with your work. (**Miss Moray** *surveys everything, then sits on a stool. Dan rushes in with large jars on a wheeled table.*)

Dan. Scuse me, but I figure I'll get the formaldehyde set up tonight.

Miss Moray. Very good, Dan.

Helen. (*noticing the dolphin is stirring*) What's the formaldehyde for?

Miss Moray. The experiment series on . . . the dolphin will . . . terminate[4] on Friday. That's why it has concerned me that you've apparently grown . . . fond . . . of the mammal.

Helen. They're gonna kill it?

---

[4]come to an end

Dan.   Gonna sharpen the handsaws now. Won't have any trouble getting through the skull on this one, no, sir. *(He exits.)*

Helen.   What for? Because it didn't say anything? Is that what they're killing it for?

Miss Moray.   Helen, no matter how lovely our intentions, no matter how lonely we are and how much we want people or animals . . . to like us . . . we have no right to endanger the genius about us. Now, we've spoken about this before. (**Helen** *is dumbfounded as* **Miss Moray** *exits.* **Helen** *gathers her equipment and looks at the dolphin, which is staring desperately at her.)*

Dolphin.   Help. *(pause)* Please help me.
(**Helen** *is so moved by the cries of the dolphin she looks ready to burst into tears as the lights go down, ending* **Act I**.*)*

ACT II

(The hall: It is the night that the dolphin is to be dissected. Elevator doors open and **Helen** *gets off, nods, and starts down the hall.* **Miss Moray** *comes to* **Helen** *at closet.)*

Miss Moray.   I hope you're well this evening.

Helen.   When they gonna kill it?

Miss Moray.   Don't say kill, Helen. You make it sound like murder. Besides, you won't have to go into the laboratory at all this evening.

Helen.   How do they kill it?

Miss Moray.   Nicotine mustard, Helen. It's very humane. They inject it.

Helen.   Maybe he's a mute.

Miss Moray.   Do you have all your paraphernalia?[5]

Helen.   Some human beings are mute, you know. Just because they can't talk we don't kill them.

Miss Moray.   It looks like you're ready to open a new box of steel wool.

Helen.   Maybe he can type with his nose. Did they try that?

Miss Moray.   Now, now, Helen—

Helen.   Miss Moray, I don't mind doing the lab.

Miss Moray.   Absolutely not! I'm placing it off limits for your own good. You're too emotionally involved.

Helen.   I can do the lab, honest. I'm not emotionally involved.

Miss Moray.   (*motioning her to the specimen room door*) Trust me, Helen. Trust me.

Helen.   (*reluctantly disappearing through the door.*) Yes, Miss Moray. (**Miss Moray** *stations herself at the desk near the elevator and begins reading her charts.* **Helen** *slips out of the specimen room and into the laboratory without being seen. The lights in the lab are out and moonlight from the window casts eerie shadows.*)

Dolphin.   Help. (**Helen** *opens the curtain. The dolphin and she look at each other.*)

Dolphin.   Help me.

Helen.   You don't need me. Just say something to them. Anything. They just need to hear you say something. . . . You want me to tell 'em? I'll tell them. I'll just say I heard you say "Help." (*pauses, then speaks with feigned cheerfulness*) I'll go tell them.

Dolphin.   Noooooooooooooooooo. (**Helen** *stops. Moves back toward tank.*)

---

[5]equipment

Helen.   They're gonna kill you!

Dolphin.   Plaaaaan.

Helen.   What?

Dolphin.   Plaaaaaaaan.

Helen.   Plan? What plan? (**Dan** *charges through the door and snaps on the light.*)

Dan.   Uh-oh. Miss Moray said she don't want you in here. (**Helen** *goes to* **Dr. Crocus**'s *desk and begins to look at various books on it.*)

Helen.   Do you know anything about a plan?

Dan.   She's gonna be mad. What plan?

Helen.   Something to do with . . . (*She indicates the dolphin.*)

Dan.   Hiya, fella!

Helen.   About the dolphin . . .

Dan.   They got an experiment book they write in.

Helen.   Where?

Dan.   I don't know.

Helen.   Find it and bring it to me in the animals' morgue. Please.

Dan.   I'll try. I'll try, but I got other things to do, you know. (**Helen** *slips out the door and makes it safely back into the specimen room.* **Dan** *rummages through the desk and finally finds the folder. He is able to sneak into the specimen room.*)

Dan.   Here. (**Helen** *grabs the folder and starts going through it.* **Dan** *turns and is about to go back out into the hall when he sees that* **Miss Moray** *has stopped reading.* **Helen** *skims through more of the folder. It is a bulky affair. She stops at a page discussing uses of dolphins.* **Miss Moray** *gets up from the desk and heads for the specimen-room door.*)

Dan.   She's coming.

Helen.   Maybe you'd better hide. Get behind the table. Here, take the book. (**Dan** *ducks down behind one of the specimen tables, and* **Helen** *starts scrubbing away.* **Miss Moray** *opens the door.*)

Miss Moray.   Perk-You-Up time, Helen. Tell Dan, please. He's in the laboratory. (**Helen** *moves to the lab door, opens it, and calls into the empty room.*)

Helen.   Perk-You-Up time.

Miss Moray.   Tell him we have ladyfingers.

Helen.   We have ladyfingers.

Miss Moray.   Such a strange thing to call a confectionery, isn't it? It's almost macabre.[6]

Helen.   Miss Moray . . .

Miss Moray.   Yes, Helen?

Helen.   I was wondering why they wanna talk with . . .

Miss Moray.   Now now now!

Helen.   I mean, supposing dolphins *did* talk?

Miss Moray.   Well, like fishing, Helen. If we could communicate with dolphins, they might be willing to herd fish for us. The fishing industry would be revolutionized.

Helen.   Is that all?

Miss Moray.   All? Heavens, no. They'd be a blessing to the human race. A blessing. They would be worshipped in oceanography. Checking the Gulf Stream . . . taking water temperatures, depths, salinity readings. To say nothing of the contributions they could make in marine biology, navigation, linguistics! Oh, Helen, it gives me the chills.

Helen.   It'd be good if they talked?

Miss Moray.   God's own blessing. (**Dan** *opens the lab doors and yells over Helen's head to* **Miss Moray**.)

-----

[6]gruesome; suggesting death

Dan. I got everything except the head vise. They can't saw through the skull bone without the head vise.

Miss Moray. Did you look on five? They had it there last week for . . . what they did to the St. Bernard. (*From the laboratory, music drifts out. They try to talk over it.*)

Dan. I looked on five.

Miss Moray. You come with me. It must have been staring you in the face. (**Dan** and **Miss Moray** *get on the elevator.*)

Miss Moray. We'll be right back, Helen. (*The doors close and* **Helen** *hurries into the laboratory. She stops just inside the door, and it is obvious that she is angry.*)

Dolphin. Booooooooook.

Helen. I looked at your book. I looked at your book all right!

Dolphin. Booooooooook.

Helen. And you want to know what I think? I don't think much of you, that's what I think.

Dolphin. Booooooooook.

Helen. Oh, shut up. Book book book book book. I'm not interested. You eat yourself silly—but to get a little fish for hungry humans is just too much for you. Well, I'm going to tell 'em you can talk. (*The dolphin moves in the tank, lets out a few warning bubbles.*)

Helen. You don't like that, eh! Well, I don't like lazy self-ish people, mammals or animals. (*The dolphin looks increasingly desperate and begins to make loud blatt and beep sounds. He struggles in the tank.*)

Helen. Cut it out—you're getting water all over the floor.

Dolphin. Booooooooook! (**Helen** *looks at the folder on the desk. She picks it up, opens it, closes it, and sets it down again.*)

Helen. I guess you don't like us. I guess you'd die rather than help us . . .

Dolphin. Hate.

Helen. I guess you do hate us . . . (*She returns to the folder.*)

Helen. (*reading*) Military implications . . . war . . . plant mines in enemy waters . . . deliver atomic warheads . . . war . . . nuclear torpedoes . . . attach bombs to submarines . . . terrorize enemy waters . . . war. . . . They're already thinking about ways to use you for war. Is that why you can't talk to them? (*pause*) What did you talk to me for? (*pause*) You won't talk to them, but you . . . you talk to me because . . . you want something . . . there's something . . . I can do?

Dolphin. Hamm . . .

Helen. What?

Dolphin. Hamm . . .

Helen. Ham? I thought you ate fish.

Dolphin. (*moving with annoyance*) Ham . . . purrrr.

Helen. Ham . . . purrrr? I don't know what you're talking about.

Dolphin. (*even more annoyed*) Ham . . . purrrr.

Helen. Ham . . . purrrr. What's a purrrr? (*Confused and scared, she returns to scrubbing the hall floor just as the doors of the elevator open, revealing* **Miss Moray, Dan,** *and* **Mr. Fridge. Dan** *pushes a dissection table loaded with shiny instruments toward the lab.*)

Miss Moray. Is the good doctor in yet?

Mr. Fridge. He's getting the nicotine mustard on nine. I'll see if he needs assistance.

Miss Moray. I'll come with you. You'd better leave now, Helen. It's time. (*She smiles and the elevator doors close.*)

Dan. (*pushing the dissection table through the lab doors*) I never left a dirty head vise. She's trying to say I left it like that.

Helen.   Would you listen a minute? Ham . . . purrrr. Do you know what a ham . . . purrrr is?

Dan.   The only hamper I ever heard of is out in the hall. (**Helen** *darts to the door, opens it, and sees the hampers at the end of the hall.*)

Helen.   The hamper!

Dan.   Kazinski left the high-altitude chamber dirty once, and I got blamed for that, too. (*He exits.*)

Helen.   (*rushing to the dolphin*) You want me to do something with the hamper. What? To get it? To put . . . you want me to put you in it? But what'll I do with you? Where can I take you?

Dolphin.   Sea . . .

Helen.   See? See what?

Dolphin.   Sea . . .

Helen.   I don't know what you're talking about. They'll be back in a minute. I don't know what to do!

Dolphin.   Sea . . . sea . . .

Helen.   See? . . . The sea! That's what you're talking about! The river . . . to the sea! (*She darts into the hall and heads for the hamper. Quickly she pushes it into the lab, and just as she gets through the doors unseen,* **Miss Moray** *gets off the elevator.*)

Miss Moray.   Helen? (*She starts down the hall. Enters the lab. The curtain is closed in front of the tank.*)

Miss Moray.   Helen? Are you here? Helen? (*She sees nothing and is about to leave when she hears a movement behind the curtain. She looks down and sees* **Helen**'s *shoes. Miss Moray moves to the curtain and pulls it open. There is* **Helen** *with her arms around the front part of the dolphin, lifting it a good part of the way out of the water.*)

Miss Moray.   Helen, what do you think you're hugging? (**Helen** *drops the dolphin back into the tank.*)

Mr. Fridge.   (*entering*) Is anything wrong, Miss Moray?

Miss Moray.   No . . . nothing wrong. Nothing at all. Just a little spilled water. (**Helen** and **Miss Moray** *grab sponges from the lab sink and begin to wipe up the water around the tank.* **Dr. Crocus** *enters and begins to fill a hypodermic syringe while* **Mr. Fridge** *expertly gets all equipment into place.* **Dan** *enters.*)

Mr. Fridge.   Would you like to get an encephalogram during the death process, Dr. Crocus?

Dr. Crocus.   Why not? (**Mr. Fridge** *begins to implant electrodes in the dolphin's head. The dolphin commences making high-pitched distress signals.*)

Miss Moray.   Come, Helen. I'll see you to the elevator. (**Miss Moray** *leads her out to the hall.* **Helen** *gets on her coat and kerchief.*)

Miss Moray.   Frankly, Helen, I'm deeply disappointed. I'd hoped that by being lenient[7] with you—and heaven knows I have been—you'd develop a heightened loyalty to our team.

Helen.   (*bursting into tears and going to the elevator*) Leave me alone.

Miss Moray.   (*softening as she catches up to her*) You really are a nice person, Helen. A very nice person. But to be simple and nice in a world where great minds are giant-stepping the micro-and macrocosms, well—one would expect you'd have the humility to yield in unquestioning awe. I truly am very fond of you, Helen, but you're fired. Call Personnel after nine A.M. (*As* **Miss Moray** *disappears into the laboratory, the record starts to play.*)

Record.   "Let me call you sweetheart,

I'm in love with you.

Let me hear you whisper . . ."

---

[7] not strict; forgiving

*(The record is roughly interrupted. Instead of getting on the elevator, **Helen** whirls around and barges into the lab.)*

Helen.   Who do you think you are? *(pause)* Who do you think you are? *(pause)* I think you're a pack of killers, that's what I think.

Miss Moray.   Doctor, I assure you this is the first psychotic[8] outbreak she's made. She did the entire brass strip . . .

Helen.   I'm very tired of being a nice person, Miss Moray. I'm going to report you to the ASPCA, or somebody, because . . . I've decided I don't like you cutting the heads off mice and sawing through skulls of St. Bernards . . . and if being a nice person is just not saying anything and letting you pack of butchers run around doing whatever you want, then I don't want to be nice anymore. *(pause)* You gotta be very stupid people to need an animal to talk before you know just from looking at it that it's saying something . . . that it knows what pain feels like. I'd like to see you all with a few electrodes in your heads. Being nice isn't any good. *(looking at dolphin)* They just kill you off if you do that. And that's being a coward. You gotta talk back. You gotta speak up against what's wrong and bad, or you can't ever stop it. At least you've gotta try. *(She bursts into tears.)*

Miss Moray.   Nothing like this has ever happened with a member of the Custodial Engineering . . . Helen, dear . . .

Helen.   Get your hands off me. *(yelling at the dolphin)* You're a coward, that's what you are. I'm going.

Dolphin.   Loooooooooveeeeeeeee. *(Everyone turns to stare at the dolphin.)*

Dolphin.   Love.

Dr. Crocus.   Get the recorder going. *(**Helen** pats the dolphin, exits. The laboratory becomes a bustle of activity.)*

─────────

[8] showing a mental disorder

Dolphin. Love . . .

Dr. Crocus. Is the tape going?

Mr. Fridge. Yes, Doctor.

Dolphin. Love . . .

Dr. Crocus. I think that woman's got something to do with this. Get her back in here.

Miss Moray. Oh, I fired her. She was hugging the mammal . . . and . . .

Dolphin. Love . . .

Dr. Crocus. Just get her. *(to* **Mr. Fridge***)* You're sure the machine's recording?

Miss Moray. Doctor, I'm afraid you don't understand. That woman was hugging the mammal . . .

Dr. Crocus. Try to get another word out of it. One more word . . .

Miss Moray. The last thing in the world I want is for our problem in Custodial Engineering to . . .

Dr. Crocus. *(furious)* Will you shut up and get that wash-woman back in here?

Miss Moray. Immediately, Doctor. *(She hurries out of the lab.* **Helen** *is at the end of the hall waiting for the elevator.)*

Miss Moray. Helen? Oh, Helen? Don't you want to hear what the dolphin has to say? He's so cute! Dr. Crocus thinks that his talking might have something to do with you. Wouldn't that be exciting? *(pause)* Please, Helen. The doctor . . .

Helen. Don't talk to me, do you mind?

Miss Moray. It was only in the heat of argument that I . . . of course, you won't be discharged. All right? Please, Helen, you'll embarrass me . . . *(The elevator doors open and* **Helen** *gets on to face* **Miss Moray.** *She looks at her a moment and then lifts her hand to press the button for the ground floor.)*

Miss Moray.   Don't you dare . . . Helen, the team needs you, don't you see? You've done so well—the brass strip, the floors. The floors have never looked so good. Ever. Helen, please. What will I do if you leave?

Helen.   Why don't you get a rug? (**Helen** *helps slam the elevator doors in* **Miss Moray**'s *face as the lights go down, ending the play.*)

REVIEWING AND INTERPRETING
Record your answers to these questions in your personal literature notebook. Follow the directions for each part.

REVIEWING   Try to complete each of these sentences without looking back at the play.

Recalling Facts   1. Helen left her former job because
   a. she had made too many mistakes to be kept on.
   b. the building had been torn down.
   c. a rug had been installed, making her job unnecessary.
   d. her bosses had decided that she was too old to do the job.

Identifying Cause and Effect   2. The first time Helen sees the dolphin, she feels concerned because
   a. she thinks that his tank is too small for him.
   b. she believes that the dolphin is frightened.
   c. the dolphin looks pale and sick.
   d. she is afraid the dolphin will attack her.

Identifying Sequence   3. After the dolphin talks to Helen for the first time, she
   a. pats it on the head and says, "That's a good boy."
   b. reports to Miss Moray that the dolphin is making a funny noise.
   c. asks it to speak to the scientists to prove it can talk.
   d. tries to put it in a hamper.

Understanding Main Ideas   4. The dolphin refuses to speak because it
   a. simply doesn't like Dr. Crocus.
   b. is afraid that its abilities will be used in wars.
   c. doesn't know human language, only dolphin language.
   d. doesn't want to help human beings catch fish.

Recognizing Literary Elements (Character)

5. Choose the character who is described by the author in this way: "The dedicated man of science who devises and presides over the weird experiments."
a. Dan
b. Mr. Fridge
c. Dr. Crocus
d. Kazinski

INTERPRETING

To complete these sentences, you may look back at the play if you'd like.

Making Inferences

6. Through what she says and does, Miss Moray makes it clear that she values employees who
a. love and respect animals.
b. ask plenty of questions.
c. think for themselves.
d. follow directions.

Analyzing

7. The dolphin probably speaks only to Helen because
a. it has decided that she might be willing to help it escape.
b. Helen knows more about dolphins than the doctor knows.
c. Helen never tries to tape-record its words.
d. the doctor is too impatient to wait for the dolphin to speak.

Predicting Outcomes

8. Now that Dr. Crocus has heard the dolphin speak, he will probably
a. set the dolphin free.
b. do many more experiments on it.
c. put the dolphin to sleep immediately.
d. give up on his experiments.

Making
Generalizations

9. With which of these statements would the dolphin be most likely to agree?
a. Keeping the world at peace is more important than saving your own life.
b. Communication with humans will lead to a wonderful future.
c. All humans are dangerous.
d. Dolphins are not as intelligent as human beings.

Understanding
Literary Elements
(Character)

10. A good way to describe Miss Moray is
a. curious and brave.
b. kind and funny.
c. intelligent and sensitive.
d. stern and narrow-minded.

Now check your answers with your teacher. Study the questions you answered incorrectly. What types of questions were they? Talk with your teacher about ways to work on those skills.

Theme

Writers often try to make their readers think about important ideas. Through their stories, poems, and plays, they explore beliefs and messages about life and its lessons. These messages or lessons are called *themes*.

Sometimes a theme teaches a clear and obvious lesson. For example, the theme of "Little Red Riding Hood" is to avoid talking to or trusting strangers. Even a little child can understand and state that theme. At other times, however, a theme is less obvious. Instead of being stated directly and clearly, the theme might be an idea or question that comes up again and again in a piece of writing. By bringing the idea up many times, the author forces you to look at the idea or question and think about your personal response to it. The author may want to share an opinion about the idea or question, or he or she may simply be saying, "Here is an important issue. Take some time and decide what you think about it."

How does an author lead you to think about a theme? He or she may set up a conflict within the story. By bringing two opposing forces together, the author can focus your attention on the issue or idea at the center of the conflict. The author also may create characters whose words and actions lead you to think a certain way or begin to examine your own opinions. In a play, the dialogue helps you understand different characters' points of view and form your own opinion.

Finally, by presenting situations and characters in a certain light, the author helps you draw on your feelings to understand the theme.

In this unit, you will look at the ways in which playwright Paul Zindel develops and helps you understand his themes:

1. He sets up conflicts that call attention to the themes.

2. He presents characters whose words and actions lead you to understand the themes.

3. He appeals to your feelings as he makes you think about the themes.

LESSON 1 THEMES AND CONFLICT

You have learned that sometimes an author's goal is to make readers think about important ideas, or themes. For example, one theme in a story might be that humans are making it difficult for wild animals to live in the American West. To bring out this theme, the author could tell the story from the animals' point of view, or he or she could tell it from a builder's point of view. A play about the conflict could begin with a wolf attacking a citizen of a growing Western town. By setting up a conflict between people and animals, the author encourages you to think about the problem and decide where you stand on the issue.

Read this part of *Let Me Hear You Whisper* to determine the central conflict in the play. Think about how this conflict leads you to understand the play's main theme.

Helen.   (*noticing the dolphin is stirring*) What's the formaldehyde for?

Miss Moray.   The experiment series on . . . the dolphin will . . . terminate on Friday. That's why it has concerned me that you've apparently grown . . . fond . . . of the mammal.

Helen.   They're gonna kill it?

Dan.   Gonna sharpen the handsaws now. Won't have any trouble getting through the skull on this one, no, sir. (*He exits.*)

Helen. What for? Because it didn't say anything? Is that what they're killing it for?

Miss Moray. Helen, no matter how lovely our intentions, no matter how lonely we are and how much we want people or animals . . . to like us . . . we have no right to endanger the genius about us. Now, we've spoken about this before. (**Helen** *is dumbfounded as* **Miss Moray** *exits.* **Helen** *gathers her equipment and looks at the dolphin, which is staring desperately at her.*)

Dolphin. Help. (*pause*) Please help me.

What two forces are in conflict here? Miss Moray believes that the dolphin is simply a tool to advance the "genius" of science. She is most interested in making the "termination" of the dolphin as easy as possible. Helen, on the other hand, is horrified to think of killing the dolphin, especially since she knows that it can feel and think, just as a human can. By bringing these two opinions together, the author makes you ask yourself questions such as, "Do humans have the right to do whatever they want with animals?" and "How far should science be able to go when it comes to animal research?"

EXERCISE 1

Read this passage from the play. Use what you have learned in this lesson to answer the questions that follow.

Helen. You don't like that, eh? Well, I don't like lazy selfish people, mammals or animals. . . . I guess you don't like us. I guess you'd die rather than help us . . .

Dolphin. Hate.

Helen. I guess you do hate us . . . (*She returns to the folder.*)

Helen. *(reading)* Military implications . . . war . . . plant mines in enemy waters . . . deliver atomic warheads . . . war . . . nuclear torpedoes . . . attach bombs to sub-marines . . . terrorize enemy waters . . . war. . . . They're already thinking about ways to use you for war. Is that why you can't talk to them? *(pause)* What did you talk to me for? *(pause)* You won't talk to them, but you . . . you talk to me because . . . you want something . . . there's something . . . I can do?

1. Why is Helen angry with the dolphin at the beginning of the passage? What does she think are the two forces in conflict at this point?

2. The contents of the folder explain why the dolphin refuses to cooperate with the scientists. What theme about human nature does the author suggest in the conflict between the dolphin and the scientists who made the plan?

Now check your answers with your teacher. Review this part of the lesson if you don't understand why an answer was incorrect.

 WRITING ON YOUR OWN 1

In this exercise you will use what you have learned in this lesson to explore two themes about a particular conflict. Follow these steps:

• Think about problems that are facing your family, school, or community. Write descriptions of at least three problems.
• For each problem, write a brief description of the forces involved in the conflict. For example, if the problem in a family is deciding what to do with money that has been inherited, the conflict may be that some family members may want to save it, while others want to spend it. Or your community may be in conflict over a new shopping mall—

one side may want to encourage growth, while the other side wants to keep the community small and quiet.
- Choose one of the conflicts. State themes that express the values that each side believes in. For example, if your community is split over the new shopping mall, one side's message or theme might be, "Too much growth makes cities less safe and peaceful." The other side's message or theme might be, "Communities should make sure that all the needs of their citizens are met."

LESSON 2 THEMES AND CHARACTERS

There is often more than one message, or theme, in any piece of writing, especially in a long work such as a play. Usually, if you listen carefully to the words of the characters in a play, you can discover most of the author's themes.

For example, how would you describe Helen's character after reading this dialogue from the play? Would you say that she is easily swayed by others' opinions, or is she a person who thinks for herself? How do you think the author feels about people such as Helen?

Miss Moray. Didn't you find Personnel pleasant?

Helen. They asked a lot of crazy questions.

Miss Moray. Oh, I'm sorry. (*pause*) For instance.

Helen. They wanted to know what went on in my head when I'm watching television in my living room and the audience laughs. They asked if I ever thought the audience was laughing at *me*.

Miss Moray. (*laughing*) My, oh, my! (*pause*) What did you tell them?

Helen. I don't have a TV.

Miss Moray. I'm sorry.

Helen. I'm not.

Helen seems to be simple, forthright, and down-to-earth. She doesn't put up with silliness, whether it comes from people who ask useless questions or television shows that are not worth watching. She doesn't mind that she is out of step with most other people. She thinks for herself and doesn't care who knows it. The author seems to admire her independent spirit. Helen's character suggests another theme of the play—the importance of making up your own mind and not being swayed by others' opinions.

EXERCISE 2

Read this dialogue between Helen and Miss Moray. Then use what you have learned in this lesson to answer the questions that follow.

Helen. Oh, yeah. . . . They chopped the heads off three hundred mice? That's horrible.

Miss Moray. You're so sensitive, Helen. Every laboratory in the country is doing this type of work. It's quite accepted.

Helen. Every laboratory cutting off mouse heads!

Miss Moray. Virtually . . .

Helen. How many laboratories are there?

Miss Moray. I don't know. I suppose at least five thousand.

Helen. Five thousand times three hundred . . . that's a lot of mouse heads. Can't you just have one lab chop off a couple and then spread the word?

Miss Moray. Now, Helen—this is exactly what I mean. You will do best not to become fond of the subject animals. When you're here a little longer you'll learn . . . well . . . there are some things you just have to accept on faith.

1. How would you describe Miss Moray, based on this dialogue?

2. How does Miss Moray feel about animals, science, and her job? Suggest one of the themes or values she seems to have learned in her life.

Now check your answers with your teacher. Review this part of the lesson if you don't understand why an answer was incorrect.

WRITING ON YOUR OWN 2

In this exercise you will use what you have learned in the lesson to analyze a character from the play and show how he illustrates a theme.

- You have already looked at the characters of Helen and Miss Moray. You know that the author has used these characters to express certain themes. For example, by looking at Helen's words and actions, you know that she believes in thinking independently and being kind to animals. Now turn your attention to Dr. Crocus and Dan.
- What messages is the author trying to convey through Dan and Dr. Crocus? To answer the question, page through the play and review what each character says and does. Jot down notes about each character on a separate sheet of paper.
- Look over your notes. Considering the words and actions of the characters, write a statement that expresses one theme or value that each character stands for and believes in.

LESSON 3   THEMES AND FEELINGS

As you read a play, your feelings help you find its themes. Pay attention to the way you feel about different characters and situations. It is no accident that you feel as you do.

From the first words of the play, the author tries to stir certain emotions within you. These emotions lead you to the themes of the play.

Read the following dialogue from the end of *Let Me Hear You Whisper*. How do you feel about Helen as you read her words? How do you feel about Miss Moray and Dr. Crocus? What techniques does the author use to make you feel this way?

> (. . . *Instead of getting on the elevator,* **Helen** *whirls around and barges into the lab.*)
>
> **Helen.**   Who do you think you *are*? (*pause*) Who do you think you are? (*pause*) I think you're a pack of killers, that's what I think.
>
> **Miss Moray.**   Doctor, I assure you this is the first psychotic outbreak she's made. She did the entire brass strip . . .
>
> **Helen.**   I'm very tired of being a nice person, Miss Moray. I'm going to report you to the ASPCA, or somebody, because . . . I've decided I don't like you cutting the heads off mice and sawing through skulls of St. Bernards . . . and if being a nice person is just not saying anything and letting you pack of butchers run around doing whatever you want, then I don't want to be nice anymore. (*pause*) You gotta be very stupid people to need an animal to talk before you know just from looking at it that it's saying something . . . that it knows what pain feels like. I'd like to see you all with a few electrodes in your heads. Being nice isn't any good. (*looking at dolphin*) They just kill you off if you do that. And that's being a coward. You gotta talk back. You gotta speak up against what's wrong and bad, or you can't ever stop it. At least you've gotta try. (*She bursts into tears.*)

If you are like most readers, you probably feel like standing up and cheering for Helen for deciding to "speak up against what's wrong and bad." Not only is she probably expressing your feelings, she is also stating the theme that the author wants to convey. Throughout the play, you have been maneuvered into Helen's corner, on the side of the captive dolphin. When Helen finally fights back you probably feel victorious—glad that the snooty Miss Moray is embarrassed and that the cold Dr. Crocus is put in his place.

The author has Helen use simple, easily understood words. She is not a fancy scientist but instead represents every ordinary person who is seeing or reading the play. The author shows how important these ideas are to Helen by making this Helen's longest speech in the play. One of the play's most important themes—the necessity for personal courage no matter the cost—is now clear.

EXERCISE 3

Read this passage in which Miss Moray fires Helen. Then use what you have learned in this lesson to answer the questions that follow.

Miss Moray.   Frankly, Helen, I'm deeply disappointed. I'd hoped that by being lenient with you—and heaven knows I have been—you'd develop a heightened loyalty to our team.

Helen.   *(bursting into tears and going to the elevator)* Leave me alone.

Miss Moray.   *(softening as she catches up to her)* You really are a nice person, Helen. A very nice person. But to be simple and nice in a world where great minds are giant-stepping the micro- and macrocosms, well—one would expect you'd have the humility to yield in unquestioning awe. I truly am very fond of you, Helen, but you're fired. Call Personnel after nine A.M.

1. What are your feelings toward Miss Moray? Have they changed in the course of the play, or have they stayed the same?

2. Throughout the play, you probably sympathize with Helen and agree with what she says. Find at least three statements or actions in the play that make you disagree with Miss Moray and what she says.

Now check your answers with your teacher. Review this part of the lesson if you don't understand why an answer was incorrect.

 WRITING ON YOUR OWN 3

In this exercise you will use what you have learned in this lesson to make the characters sympathetic to the other side of the theme's argument. Follow these steps:

- Not everyone agrees that using animals in experiments is wrong. Some people feel that risking animals' lives is better than risking human lives. Describe changes you would make to the play to make the audience more willing to accept this point of view.
- First look at the setting of the play. Where else could the play be set to make animal experiments look like a good practice? Write a short description of the new setting.
- Then think about the characters. How would you change Helen, Miss Moray, and Dr. Crocus? Would you add any new characters? How would you change the Dolphin? What would you have the characters say and do? Make a list of all the changes you would make to the play to express a theme that is sympathetic to science and animal experimentation.

DISCUSSION GUIDES

1. The fate of the friendly dolphin is left unclear at the end of this play. With a classmate, write a new ending for the play that shows what happens to the dolphin. After you have finished, ask some volunteers to help you read the new ending to the rest of the class.

2. As you probably know, animal testing causes much controversy in real life, not just in plays. People who defend it argue that experimenting with animals can bring untold benefits to the human race without sacrificing any human lives. Those who are against it believe that it is needlessly cruel to innocent animals. With a small group of classmates, survey twenty people to find out where they stand on this issue. Then report your survey results to the rest of the class. Do the different groups' results reveal different opinions? Which opinions seem to be the most and least popular?

3. The importance of communication is a central theme of this play. With a partner, make a list of at least five jobs that require effective communication skills. Fill in a chart like the one below, listing both the job and the reason good communication skills are important.

Job	Why good communication skills are important
Trial Lawyer	The jury needs to hear and understand evidence showing why a person is innocent or guilty.

WRITE A DIALOGUE ON A THEME

In this unit you have seen how authors use conflicts, characters, and feelings to develop and express themes. In the writing exercises in this unit, you have used some of those same techniques. Now it is time to express a theme in an original dialogue. Follow the steps below.

If you have questions about the writing process, refer to Using the Writing Process (page 261).

- Assemble all the writing assignments you completed in this unit. They should include 1) a chart listing lessons you have learned at home, at school, from friends, and in your community; 2) conflicting themes about a particular conflict; 3) statements that express themes that Dan and Dr. Crocus stand for; and 4) a list of changes you would like to make to the play.
- After reviewing your assignments, choose a single theme to present in a dialogue. It can be a theme that you suggested in the first writing exercise, or it can be a new theme.
- Write a short description of each of your characters, as was done at the beginning of *Let Me Hear You Whisper*. Describe the setting briefly. Set up the format of the dialogue as it is done for the plays in this book.
- Try to make the dialogue sound as realistic as possible. The words should sound natural, just as the characters would sound if they were conversing in real life. Make sure the theme you have chosen comes through their words clearly.
- Read your dialogue aloud to friends or family members. As you read, mark words or phrases that don't sound believable so you can revise them later. Ask your listeners to identify the theme that they see in the dialogue. If the theme isn't clear enough, or if additions and corrections are needed, revise your dialogue.
- Proofread your dialogue for spelling, grammar, punctuation, capitalization, and formatting errors. If possible, have a classmate or classmates help you present your dialogue to the class.

Turning a Short Story into a Play

Rip Van Winkle

by Washington Irving

adapted by Adele Thane

INTRODUCTION

**ABOUT THE
SELECTION**

The selection you are about to read is a modern stage adaptation of a 200-year-old short story that was based on an even older story. Although that older story was a German folktale, Washington Irving set his version in his home state of New York. The villagers in Irving's version are all descendants of the original Dutch settlers of the Hudson River Valley area. The first part of the play version takes place shortly before the American Revolution, and the last scene occurs not long after it.

**ABOUT THE
AUTHORS**

Washington Irving (1783–1859) was one of the first American writers to become famous in Europe as well as the United States. He was also, at various times, a lawyer, a businessman, and a diplomat. Irving was born in New York City, attended school until he was 15, and later studied law.

While still in his teens, Irving won notice for his satirical writings. In 1809 he dropped his law practice and wrote *A History of New York from the Beginning of the World to the*

End of the Dutch Dynasty, a comic masterpiece commonly called *Knickerbocker's History of New York.* In 1815 he went to England on business, but while there he began writing full-time. Within five years, he had published *The Sketch Book of Geoffrey Crayon, Gent.,* which included his two greatest works: "Rip Van Winkle" and "The Legend of Sleepy Hollow." He didn't return to New York until 1832, after traveling throughout Europe and serving as a diplomat to Spain, writing wherever he went. His works include collections of short stories and folklore, histories, and a biography of George Washington.

(Lillian) Adele Thane has had a long and varied career in theater. She was born in Massachusetts, attended schools there, and spent most of her acting and directing career with theater groups in that state. During World War II, she was a USO (United Services Organization) entertainer in hospitals and camps for three years. She became associated with children's theater in 1948 as actor, instructor, and director, both of stage performances and television plays for children. By 1952 she was producing children's plays that she had written by adapting folktales and other children's fiction to the stage. Many of her plays have been published in books and magazines.

ABOUT THE LESSONS	The lessons that follow *Rip Van Winkle* compare two versions of the same story—the play and the original short story. In other lessons in this book, the focus has been on the special characteristics of a play. You have looked at how dialogue, scenery, characters, action, and other elements tell the play's story in a unique way. In this unit you will examine what happens when a short story is rewritten into play form. What can move from the page to the stage? What must change? What is gained and lost in the translation?

WRITING: DEVELOPING AN ADAPTATION

As you will see in the course of this unit, adapting a short story for the stage can involve making choices: cutting what is not needed and adding what is missing. You can get a taste of this process by turning a familiar folktale or fairy tale into a one-act play. During the next several writing exercises, you will build characters, scenery, and dialogue from those parts of the original that can be adapted. You will add, delete, or rearrange events in the story to create a high-interest plot. You will apply everything you have learned about the elements and nature of plays. The following steps will get you started:

- List at least three fairy tales or folktales with which you are familiar. They can involve people, animals, or other beings. Each tale should have from one to four settings and from two to ten characters.
- What audience would you like to write for—children, your own age group, another group? What purpose would you have in mind—to teach, to entertain, to provoke serious conversations? Are all the tales on your list equally good for all situations? Write the title of each play at the top of a sheet of paper. For each title, write some notes about the play's purpose and audience.
- How would you advertise a play version of each of the tales on your list? What scene(s) would you illustrate on a poster? What type of musical background would you use in a radio ad—classical music, rap, fast or slow, loud or soft? On the sheet of paper for each title, sketch or describe your ideas for print and/or radio ads.
- Keep your notes handy as you work through the unit. They will help you make your final choices about the elements of your play and write your adaptation.

The questions below will help you become aware of some of the similarities and differences in the two presentations of *Rip Van Winkle*. As you read the play, keep these questions in mind:

- In addition to using dialogue from the short story as dialogue in the play, how can a playwright pick up material from the short story?
- Consider what a short story can do that a play cannot, and vice versa. Where would you look for differences between play and short story forms of this tale?
- Does the play version of *Rip Van Winkle* effectively capture the main ideas of the short story?

Rip Van Winkle

by Washington Irving

adapted by Adele Thane

---

[1] owner

SETTING

SCENE 1

Time: *Early autumn, a few years before the Revolutionary War.*

Setting: *A village in the Catskill Mountains. At left, there is an inn with a sign,* King George Tavern, *and a picture of King George III. A British Union Jack*[2] *hangs on flagpole. At right are a tree and a well.*

At rise: Nicholas Vedder, Derrick Van Bummel, Brom Dutcher, *and* **Peter Vanderdonk** *are seated aside the tavern.* **Vedder** *is sprawled back in his chair.* **Dutcher** *and* **Vanderdonk** *are at table, playing checkers.* **Van Bummel** *is reading aloud from a paper. From time to time, a rumble of thunder can be heard in the distance.*

Van Bummel. *(reading)* ". . . and it has been learned that Massachusetts favors a Stamp Act Congress to be held in New York to protest English taxation in the Colonies."

Dutcher. *(looking up from game)* Good! It's high time we did something about this English taxation.

Vanderdonk. Taxes and more taxes! The English are a pack of rascals with their hands in our pockets.

Van Bummel. There's even a revenue stamp on our newspapers. One of these days the people here in the American Colonies will revolt, you mark my words.

Vedder. *(pointing off right as a merry whistle is heard)* Well, here comes one man who is not troubled by these problems—Rip Van Winkle. (**Rip Van Winkle** *enters, holding bucket and gun. He props gun against tree at right, then crosses to men.)*

---

[2] flag of the United Kingdom; Before 1776 it was the flag of England and all her colonies, including those in America.

Rip.   Good afternoon, Nick Vedder—Brom—Peter. (*to* **Van Bummel**) Good afternoon, Mr. Schoolmaster. (*They return his greeting. There is a loud rumble of thunder.*) Just listen to that, will you!

Dutcher.   We're in for a storm.

Vedder.   Sit down, Rip. Derrick is reading us the news.

Vanderdonk.   How about a game of checkers, Rip?

Rip.   (*hesitating*) I don't know. Dame Van Winkle sent me for a bucket of water, but—maybe *one* game. (*Sets down bucket and draws stool up to table. Suddenly* **Dame Van Winkle**'s *voice is heard.*)

Dame Van Winkle.   (*calling from off right*) Rip! R-i-p! Rip Van Winkle!

Rip.   Oh, my galligaskins![3] It's my wife! (**Dame Van Winkle** *enters with a broom and crosses directly to* **Rip.**)

Dame Van Winkle.   So this is how you draw water from the well! Sitting around with a lot of lazy, good-for-nothing loafers. (*tries to hit* **Rip** *with broom*) Pick up that bucket, you dawdling Dutchman, and fill it with water!

Rip.   (*snatching up bucket and dodging out of the way*) Hey there, Dame, I'm not an old rug to be beaten with a broomstick.

Dame Van Winkle.   An old rug would be more use than you. At least it would keep our feet warm in winter, which is more than you can do. Little you care that your family is starving and the cow is gone.

Rip.   The cow gone?

Dame Van Winkle.   Aye, the cow is gone and the cabbage trampled down. When are you going to mend the fence?

Rip.   I'll mend the fence—tomorrow.

---

[3] leggings or loose trousers that end just below the knees

Dame Van Winkle. Tomorrow, tomorrow! All your work is going to be done tomorrow! (**Rip** *goes to well at right as she starts off right, still talking.*) You show enough energy when there's a husking bee[4] or an errand to run for the neighbors, but here at home . . . (*She exits.* **Rip** *lowers bucket into well. Men rise to go into tavern.*)

Vedder. Poor Rip! His wife has the sharpest tongue in the Hudson Valley.

Dutcher. What would you do, Derrick, if you had a wife like Van Winkle's?

Van Bummel. War could be no worse. I would enlist. (*They laugh and exit through door of tavern.* **Rip** *turns to leave, then stops and smiles, as* **Judy, Luke, Meenie,** *holding a kite, and* **Jacob,** *carrying a bow, run in, left.*)

Children. (*ad lib[5]*) There he is! There's Rip Van Winkle! (*etc. They surround him, chattering excitedly.*)

Judy. Hello, Father. I've brought some of my friends.

Rip. Glad to see you, children.

Jacob. (*holding out bow*) Rip, there's something wrong with my bow. Every time I try to shoot, the cord slips. (**Rip** *takes bow, draws knife from pocket and pretends to cut notch for cord deeper.*)

Rip. There, Jacob, try that, and see if it doesn't work.

Jacob. (*pretending to shoot*) Yes, it's all right now.

Meenie. (*holding out kite*) My kite won't stay up, Rip.

Rip. (*taking off part of tail*) Now it will, Meenie. (*hands kite to* **Meenie**)

Luke. Rip, will you see what's the matter with my whistle? (*hands* **Rip** *a whistle*)

---

[4] gathering of friends and neighbors to take the dry outer leaves off of corn

[5] make up words that are not in the script

Rip.   (*examining it*) You haven't whittled[6] it right there, Luke. Here, I'll fix it for you. (*He sits on bench and begins to whittle.*)

Judy.   Tell us a story, Father!

Luke.   Yes, you tell better stories than anybody else in the Catskills. (*Children sit in circle around* **Rip.**)

Rip.   What shall it be about?

Meenie.   Witches and goblins! (*Thunder is heard.*)

Judy.   Oh, Father, listen to the thunder!

Rip.   Why, don't you know what that is, Judy? That's Hendrik Hudson[7] and his famous crew, playing ninepins[8] up in the mountains. (*More thunder is heard.*)

Meenie.   Oh, What a noise they make!

Rip.   Yes, they are jolly fellows. They sail the wide sea over in their ship the *Half-Moon*, then every twenty years they come back to the Catskills.

Jacob.   What do they do that for?

Rip.   Oh, old Hendrik Hudson likes to revisit the country he discovered and keep an eye over his river, the Hudson.

Jacob.   I wish I could see Hendrik Hudson and his crew.

Rip.   Peter Vanderdonk says his father saw them once, playing at ninepins up in the hills. (*Loud peal of thunder is heard.*) Listen to the balls rolling! That must be Hendrik Hudson himself, the Flying Dutchman! (**Dame Van Winkle** *enters with broom.*)

Dame Van Winkle.   So! Here you are, telling stories without a word of truth in 'em! Oh, *I* could tell a story or two myself—about a shiftless[9] husband who does nothing but

---

[6] cut with a knife or make an object from wood by cutting with a knife

[7] Dutch name for the English explorer Henry Hudson

[8] game similar to the modern sport of bowling

[9] lazy; unable to accomplish anything

whittle and whistle. Judy, you go and ask Dame Vedder for an armful of wood. Your father is too busy spinning yarns to split wood for *our* fire. (**Judy** *goes off behind tavern.*) As for the rest of you, go home if you have any homes. (*She sweeps children off stage with broom.*) Get along! Begone, all of you! (*With arms akimbo,*[10] *she faces* **Rip**.) Well, what do you have to say for yourself? (**Rip** *shrugs, shakes his head.*) Nothing as usual. (**Rip** *goes to tree for his gun.*) What are you getting your gun for? Going off to the mountains, no doubt. Anything to keep you out of the house.

Rip.   (*good-naturedly*) Well, wife, you have often told me— *my* side of the house is the *outside*. Where's my dog? Where's Wolf?

Dame Van Winkle.   Wolf is tied up in the cellar. That dog tracked up my kitchen floor right after I'd finished scrubbing it. Well, if you're going hunting, go, and don't come back until you bring something for supper.

Judy.   (*Re-entering from up left, her arms full of logs.*) But it's going to rain.

Dame Van Winkle.   (*taking wood*) Pooh! Your father won't get as wet as we will in the house, with the roof leaking and the windows broken. You hurry home now. And bring that bucket of water, too. (**Dame Van Winkle** *starts right, but* **Judy** *stays behind with* **Rip**.)

Rip.   (*calling after his wife*) Wife, turn Wolf loose when you get home. (**Dame Van Winkle** *looks back angrily, tosses her head, and exits right.*)

Judy.   Father, where will you go if it rains?

Rip.   I'll find a place. Don't worry, Judy. Remember your little song? Come, we'll sing it together. (*They sing an appropriate folksong, such as* "Oh, Dear, What Can the Matter Be?")

---

[10] with hands on hips and elbows bent outward

Judy. (*hugging* **Rip**) Oh, Father, I hope you have wonderful luck. Then Mother won't be so cross.

Rip. I don't blame her for being cross with me sometimes. I guess I don't do much work around here. But I'm going to do better, Judy. I'm going to do all the jobs your mother has been after me to do.

Dame Van Winkle. (*calling from off*) Judy! Judy!

Rip. There's your mother. I'd better be off. Goodbye, Judy, dear. (*He walks left, whistling.*) Come, Wolf! Come, boy! (*A dog's bark is heard off left, as* **Rip** *turns, waves to* **Judy**, *and exits.*)

Judy. (*waving*) Goodbye, Father. (**Luke** *enters right and joins* **Judy** *as loud crash of thunder is heard.*) Oh, Luke, listen to that thunder!

Luke. It's only Hendrik Hudson's men playing ninepins. Don't be scared, Judy.

Judy. I'm not—that is, not very.

Dame Van Winkle. (*calling from off*) Judy! Ju-*dee*!

Luke. You'd better go in or you'll catch it. Your mother is getting awfully free with her broomstick lately. Here. I'll carry your bucket for you.

(*They exit right. Curtain.*)

Scene 2

Time: *Later the same afternoon.*

Setting: *A forest glade, high in the Catskill Mountains. There are tree stumps at right center and a large bush at far left. Scene may be played before the curtain.*

At rise: Rip, *carrying his gun, enters left, dragging his feet wearily. He sinks down on stump.*

Rip. Whew! That was a climb! All the way up the mountain. How peaceful it is up here. No one to scold me, no one to wave a broomstick. Ah, me! (*sighs contentedly*) I wonder where Wolf is. Wolf! Here, boy! (*He whistles and a dog barks off left.*) That's it, Wolf, sic 'em! I hope we get something this time. We can't go home until we do. (*Loud crash of thunder is heard.*) That thunder sounds much louder up here in the mountains than down in the valley.

Voice.   (*calling from off, high-pitched, like a bird-call*) Rip Van Winkle! (**Rip** *looks around wondrously.*) Rip Van Winkle!

Rip.   (*rising*) Somebody is calling me.

Voice.   (*off*) Rip Van Winkle!

Rip.   Is it Dame Van Winkle? No—she would never follow me up here. (*Sound of a ship's bell is heard from off right.*) What was that? (*Bell rings again.*) A ship's bell! But how can that be? A ship? Up here in the mountains? (*He gazes off right, in astonishment.*) It *is* a ship! Look at it! Sails all set—a Dutch flag at the masthead. (*Ship's bell is heard again, fainter.*) There, it's gone. I must have imagined it. (**1st Sailor**, *with a keg on his back, enters right and goes to center, as* **Rip** *watches him in amazement.*) By my galligaskins, what a funny little man! And how strangely he's dressed. Such old-fashioned clothes! (**1st Sailor** *stops at center.* **Rip** *goes to meet him.*) Hello, old Dutchman. That keg looks heavy. Let me carry it for you. (*He takes keg.*) By golly, it *is* heavy! Why did you bring this keg all the way up here to the top of the mountain? And who are you, anyhow?

1st Sailor.   (*gruffly*) Don't ask questions. Set it down over there. (*He points left to a spot beside bush.*)

Rip.   (*obeying cheerfully*) Anything to oblige. (**Hendrik Hudson** *and* **Sailors** *enter, noisily, carrying bowling balls, ninepins, and a drum.* **2nd Sailor** *has a burlap bag containing mugs.* **Rip** *turns to* **1st Sailor.**) Why, bless my soul! Here are a lot of little fellows just like yourself. (*To* **Sailors**, *as they gather at center.*) Who are you?

Sailors.   (*shouting*) Hendrik Hudson and his merry crew!

Hudson.   (*stepping forward*) Set up the ninepins, men, and we'll have a game. (**3rd** *and* **4th Sailors** *set up at extreme right.* **Hudson** *speaks to* **1st Sailor**.) You there, fill up the flagons![11] (**2nd Sailor** *opens sack and passes out mugs.* **Hudson** *turns to* **Rip**.) Now then, Rip Van Winkle, will you drink with us?

Rip.   Why, yes, thank you, Captain Hudson. I'm quite thirsty after my long climb up the mountain. (*mugs are filled from keg*)

2nd Sailor.   (*raising mug in toast*) To Hendrik Hudson, the *Half-Moon*, and its merry crew!

All.   (*as they raise mugs*) To Hendrik Hudson, the *Half-Moon*, and its merry crew!

Rip.   (*lifting his mug*) Well, gentlemen, here's to your good health. May you live long and prosper. (**Rip** *drinks and smacks his lips.*) Ah! This is the best drink I ever tasted, but it makes me feel very sleepy. (**Hudson** *and* **Sailors** *begin to bowl. As they roll the balls, thunder increases.* **Rip** *yawns.*) Ho, hum! I can't keep my eyes open. I guess I'll lie down—(*Carrying his gun, he goes behind bush at left, and lies down out of sight.* **Note**: *Unseen by audience,* **Rip** *goes offstage for costume change and returns in time for his awakening.*)

Hudson.   (*to* **Sailors**) Now, men, let's stop our game of ninepins, and have a merry dance. Then we'll be off, to return again in twenty years. (**2nd Sailor** *beats drum, and* **Sailors** *dance. At end of dance,* **1st Sailor** *points to bush where* **Rip** *is sleeping.*)

---

[11] container for liquids

1st Sailor. Look! Rip Van Winkle is asleep.

Hudson. Peace be with the poor fellow. He needs to take a good long rest from his nagging wife. (*They quietly gather up ninepins, balls, mugs, keg, etc., then tiptoe offstage. Lights dim to indicate passage of twenty years; recorded music may be played. When lights come up,* **Rip** *is heard yawning behind bush; then he stands up with great difficulty. He limps to center, carrying a rusty gun. His clothes are shabby, and he has a long white beard.*)

Rip. (*groaning*) Ouch! My back! It's so stiff. And my legs—just like pokers. My, my, but I'm shaky! I feel as if I'd grown to be an old man overnight. It must be rheumatism coming on. Oh, won't I have a blessed time with Dame Van Winkle if I'm laid up with rheumatism. Well, I'd better get along home. (*He looks at gun.*) Why, this rusty old thing is not my gun! Somebody has played a trick on me. (*suddenly recollecting*) It's that Hendrik Hudson and his men! They've stolen my gun, and left this rusty one for me! (*He puts his hand to his head.*) Another scolding in store from my wife. (*whistles*) Wolf! Here, Wolf! Have those scamps stolen my dog, too? He'd never leave me. (*whistles again*) Come on, old boy! Maybe he found it too cold and went home to be warmed by his mistress's broomstick. Well, I will follow after and get my hot welcome, too.

(*He shoulders rusty gun and totters off. Curtain.*)

Scene 3

Time: *Twenty years after Scene 1.*

Setting: *Same as Scene 1, except that sign above inn door reads:* Union Hotel—Proprietor, **Jonathan Doolittle.** *A picture of George Washington has replaced that of King George III. Washington's name is printed below picture and an American* *flag hangs on pole.*

At rise: Orator *is standing on bench, haranguing a crowd of* **Townspeople.**

Orator.   Remember the Boston Tea Party! Remember Bunker Hill! Who saved this country? Who is the father of this country?

Townspeople.   (*ad lib*) George Washington! Washington for President! (*etc. They sing "Yankee Doodle."*)

Father and I went down to camp

Along with Captain Good'in,

There we saw the men and boys

As thick as hasty puddin'.

Yankee Doodle keep it up,

Yankee Doodle Dandy,

Mind the music and the step

And with the girls be handy.

(**Rip** *enters, followed by* **Children,** *who laugh and jeer at him.*)

Children.   (*ad lib*) Look at him! He looks like a scarecrow! Where did you come from, Daddy Long-legs? Where did you get that gun? (*etc.* **Rip** *and* **Children** *go to center.* **1st Child** *stands in front of* **Rip,** *and moves hand as if stroking beard.*)

1st Child.   Billy goat, billy goat! (**Children** *begin stroking imaginary beard until* **Rip** *does the same.*)

Rip.   (*amazed*) By my galligaskins, what's this? I didn't have a beard last night. (**Children** *laugh and mock him.*)

Orator.   (*to* **Rip**) What do you mean by coming here at election time with a gun on your shoulder and a mob at your heels? Do you want to cause a riot?

Rip.   Oh, no, sir! I am a quiet man and a loyal subject of King George!

Children and Townspeople. *(shouting, ad lib)* A spy! Away with him! Lock him up. *(etc.)*

Jonathan Doolittle. *(stepping forward)* Hold on a minute! *(to Rip)* Aren't you a supporter of Washington for President?

Rip. *(puzzled)* Eh? Supporter of Washington? *(shaking his head, bewildered)* I don't understand. I mean no harm. I only want to find my friends. They were here at the tavern yesterday.

Doolittle. Who are these friends of yours? Name them.

Rip. *(hesitantly)* Well, one is the landlord—

Doolittle. I am the landlord of this hotel—Jonathan Doolittle.

Rip. Why, what happened to Nicholas Vedder?

1st Woman. *(pushing her way out of the crowd)* Nicholas Vedder? Why, he's dead and gone these eighteen years.

Rip. No, no, that's impossible! Where's Brom Dutcher? And the schoolmaster, Van Bummel—?

1st Man. Brom Dutcher was killed in the war at Stony Point.

2nd Man. And Van Bummel went off to war, too. He became a great general, and now he's in Congress.

Rip. War? What war?

2nd Man. Why, the war we fought against England, and won, of course.

Rip. I don't understand. Am I dreaming? Congress? Generals? What's happened to me?

Doolittle. *(impatiently)* Now, we've had enough of this nonsense. Who are you, anyway? What is your name?

Rip. *(utterly confused)* I don't know. I mean, I was Rip Van Winkle yesterday, but today—

Doolittle. Don't try to make sport of us, my man!

Rip. Oh, indeed, I'm not, sir. I was myself last night, but I fell asleep on the mountain, and Hendrik Hudson and his crew changed my gun, and everything's changed, and I'm changed, and I can't tell what my name is, or who I am! (**Townspeople** *exchange glances, nod knowingly, and tap their foreheads.*)

2nd Man. (*shaking his head*) Hendrik Hudson, he says! Poor chap. He's mad. Let's leave him alone.

Rip. (*in great distress*) Isn't there anybody here who knows who I am?

2nd Woman. (*soothingly*) Why, you're just yourself, old man. Who else do you think you could be? (**Judith Gardenier** *enters from left, leading* **Little Rip** *by the hand. He hangs back, whimpering.*)

Judith. Hush, Rip!

Rip. (*turning in surprise*) Rip? Who said Rip?

Judith. Why, I did. I was just telling my little boy to be quiet.

Rip. (*scanning her face*) And what is your name, my good woman?

Judith. My name is Judith, sir.

Rip. Judith! (*in great excitement*) And your father—what was his name?

Judith. Ah, poor man, his name was Rip Van Winkle. It's twenty years since he went away from home. We never heard from him again.

Rip. (*staggered*) Twenty years!

Judith. Yes. His dog came back without him. I was a little girl then.

Rip. And your mother—where is she?

Judith. My mother is dead, sir.

Rip. Well, peace be with her soul. Did you love your father, Judith?

Judith. With all my heart. All the children in the village loved him, too.

Rip. Then look at me. Look closely, my dear Judy. I am your father.

Judith. (*incredulously*) You? My father?

Rip.   We used to sing a little song together, remember? (*sings a few lines of folksong sung in* **Scene 1**)

Judith.   (*slowly*) Yes, my father used to sing that song with me, but many people know it.

Rip.   Do you remember, Judy, that I told you the story of how Hendrik Hudson and his crew played ninepins in the mountains just before I went off hunting with Wolf?

Judith.   (*excitedly*) Yes! And Wolf *was* our dog's name! Oh, Father, is it really you?

Rip.   (*hugging her*) Yes, my little Judy—young Rip Van Winkle once, old Rip Van Winkle now. (**Townspeople** *talk excitedly among themselves.*)

Judith.   Dearest Father, come home with me. Luke and I will take good care of you.

Rip.   Luke?

Judith.   Luke Gardenier, my old playmate. You used to make whistles for him and take him fishing. We were married when he came back from the war.

Rip.   Ah, the war. There is so much I have to catch up with.

Judith.   You will have plenty of time to do that—and you must tell us what happened to you.

Rip.   Maybe you won't believe what happened to me, Judy. It was all so strange. (*They start off left. Loud clap of thunder is heard and they pause.* **Rip** *turns front and shakes his fist.*) Oh, no you don't, Hendrik Hudson! You won't get me back up there again.

(*Another roll of thunder that sounds like a deep rumble of laughter is heard. Curtain.*)

THE END

REVIEWING AND INTERPRETING

Record your answers to these questions in your personal literature notebook. Follow the directions for each part.

REVIEWING

Try to complete each of these sentences without looking back at the play.

Understanding Main Ideas

1. Of the following statements, the one most likely to be true is that
   a. Rip became shiftless after his wife nagged him endlessly.
   b. if Rip had married a happier woman, he would have been a harder worker.
   c. if Rips' wife had been nicer, Rip would not have been friendly to the children.
   d. Rip would have been the same with any wife or no wife at all.

Identifying Sequence

2. Rip falls asleep in the mountains
   a. before dreaming about meeting Hendrik Hudson and his men.
   b. after Nicholas Vedder's death.
   c. after drinking from the keg Hudson's men brought with them.
   d. after playing ninepins with Hudson and his men.

Identifying Cause and Effect

3. Judith comes to believe that Rip is her father because
   a. Rip recounts their last conversation and mentions his dog's name.
   b. Rip sings lines from a song that they sang together years before.
   c. Rip looks just the way Judith remembers him.
   d. Judith thinks Rip's story is so crazy that it must be true.

Recalling Facts

4. During her father's absence, Judith marries
  a. Peter Vanderdonk.
  b. her childhood friend Meenie.
  c. Luke Gardenier.
  d. her childhood friend Jacob.

Recognizing the Elements of a Play (Staging)

5. To present the three scenes of this play, you would need
  a. one basic set and a few props that change from scene to scene.
  b. two basic sets and a few props that change from scene to scene.
  c. three very different sets and no props at all.
  d. three very different sets and a few props that change from scene to scene.

INTERPRETING

To complete these sentences, you may look back at the play if you'd like.

Making Inferences

6. Hudson invites Rip to share a drink with him and his men. Later he says about Rip, "He needs to take a good long rest from his nagging wife." From these facts, we can suppose that Hudson
  a. was surprised that Rip had such a strong reaction to the drink.
  b. knew the drink would make Rip sleep for a long time.
  c. had no concept of time.
  d. would have taken Rip with him if he had stayed awake.

Predicting Outcomes

7. After Rip moves in with his daughter, the children in the village will probably
  a. be afraid of him because he's a lunatic.
  b. become friends with him, as children did twenty years before.
  c. continue to laugh and jeer at him.
  d. lose interest in him altogether.

Making
Generalizations

8. The continuing popularity of this story reminds us that
   a. you can fool all of the people some of the time, and some of the people all of the time, but not all of the people all of the time.
   b. most people wish they could sleep for twenty years.
   c. most people enjoy a story that mixes humor, imagination, and a little truth.
   d. all married couples have problems getting along.

Analyzing

9. Skeptics in Rip's town might suspect that Rip had run away from his wife and made up the tale of meeting Hendrik Hudson to hide his cowardice. Arguments supporting this theory include the fact that
   a. he did not return until after his wife died.
   b. Rip loved his little daughter very much.
   c. he returned wearing the same clothes and carrying the same gun as people had worn twenty years earlier.
   d. his old friends in town felt sorry for him.

Understanding
Literary Elements
(Dialogue)

10. A phrase Rip uses that suggests a setting of long ago is
   a. "I'm not an old rug."
   b. "Oh, my galligaskins!"
   c. "Such old-fashioned clothes!"
   d. ". . . *my* side of the house is the *outside.*"

Now check your answers with your teacher. Study the questions you answered incorrectly. What types of questions were they? Talk with your teacher about ways to work on those skills.

Turning a Short Story into a Play

Frequently, writers are so entertained by a short story that they wish to share it with others. They decide to turn the short story into a play for a larger audience. So they turn the conversations of the story into play dialogue, they write stage directions to detail the actions described in the story, and they create scenery that matches the settings described in the story. Then they have actors act out the short story as a play.

Does this approach work? Does it produce an exciting, entertaining play? Not necessarily. The simple truth is that a good play is more than a short story with actors and scenery. Usually, the writer who adapts the short story must make additions and changes to the original story when he or she shifts the words, actions, and ideas from a short story onto a stage.

In these lessons, you will compare the play of *Rip Van Winkle* with passages from the original short story by Washington Irving. You will search for similarities and differences and see how Adele Thane applied the following principles as she adapted Irving's short story to play form:

1. Thane makes her characters say words from the story and act out movements described in it. Her stage directions also describe scenes or special effects that are mentioned in the story.

2. She changes or leaves out parts of the short story that would not work well on stage.

3. Even though she follows the words and ideas of the original story closely, she treats her play as a separate piece of writing from the original.

LESSON 1 | MAKING USE OF WHAT'S IN THE STORY

Two writers want to include the same scene in their writing: One day, all the members of a family wake up at 3 A.M. because of a raging storm. The short story writer writes:

> *At 3 A.M., a violent rainstorm woke the entire Malloy family. Little Megan leaped from bed and ran into her mother in the hall.*
> *"Mom, I'm scared!" Megan cried.*

The playwright, however, begins by writing a description of the setting on stage: the dim interior of a house, perhaps with windows through which lightning flashes can be seen. In stage directions, the playwright asks for background sounds of heavy rain and thunder. Finally, the playwright describes the entrance of characters dressed in robes and pajamas and lets them talk.

The same information is presented to the audience in both situations, but the playwright uses more than the short-story writer's words. Scenery, props, lighting, sound effects, costumes, and actions are all added to the dialogue to paint a complete picture of what is happening.

Read this passage from Washington Irving's short story "Rip Van Winkle." Then review pages 230 to 234 of the play. What information in the original story has been used in the play? Does the information appear in dialogue, scenery, or some other element of the play?

> *In that same village, and in one of these very houses (which, to tell the precise truth, was sadly time-worn and weather-beaten), there lived many years since, while the country was yet a province of Great Britain, a simple good-natured fellow, of the name of Rip Van Winkle. He was a descendant of the Van Winkles who figured so gallantly in the chivalrous days of Peter Stuyvesant, and accompanied him to the siege of Fort Christina. He*

inherited, however, but little of the martial [warlike] char-acter of his ancestors. I have observed that he was a sim-ple good-natured man; he was, moreover, a kind neighbor, and an obedient hen-pecked husband. . . .

Certain it is, that he was a great favorite among all the good wives of the village. . . . The children of the village, too, would shout with joy whenever he approached. He assisted at their sports, made their playthings, taught them to fly kites and shoot marbles, and told them long stories of ghosts, witches, and Indians. Whenever he went dodging about the village, he was surrounded by a troop of them, hanging on his skirts, clambering on his back, and playing a thousand tricks on him with impunity; and not a dog would bark at him throughout the neighbor-hood.

The great error in Rip's composition was an insupera-ble aversion to all kinds of profitable labor. . . .

The story says that this incident occurs "while the country was yet a province of Great Britain." The audience of the play learns this fact two ways. First, the scenery includes such props as a British flag, a tavern named after a king, and a picture of the king on the tavern. Second, the men at the tavern have a conversation about problems of the colonists before the Revolution, a conversation that did not happen in the story.

Notice how the play introduces its main character through Vedder's dialogue, "Well, here comes one man who is not troubled by these problems—Rip Van Winkle." That Rip is henpecked is shown in two ways. First, his wife appears in the scene and yells at him, gives him a chore, and tries to hit him with a broom. Also, the brief conversation between Vedder and Dutcher after Dame Van Winkle leaves the scene implies both men are aware of her hen-pecking! The idea that Rip has a strong dislike, or aversion, "to all kinds of prof-itable labor" is made clear by Rip's response to Dame Van

Winkle's report that the cow is gone because of a broken fence: he says he'll get around to fixing it "tomorrow."

Reread the short story's description of Rip's relationship to the village children. Then compare those sentences with the scene between Rip and the children. Notice how the playwright picks up details from the story and fleshes them out with specific children. In these ways, she adds scenery, characters, dialogue, and actions to present important ideas from the short story.

EXERCISE 1

Read the following passage and compare it with the beginning of Scene 2 (pages 235–236). Then use what you have learned in this lesson to answer the questions that follow the passage.

> *As he was about to descend, he heard a voice from a distance, hallooing, "Rip Van Winkle! Rip Van Winkle!" He looked round, but could see nothing but a crow winging its solitary flight across the mountain. He thought his fancy must have deceived him, and turned again to descend, when he heard the same cry ring through the still evening air; "Rip Van Winkle! Rip Van Winkle!" . . . . Rip . . . looked anxiously in the same direction, and perceived a strange figure slowly toiling up the rocks, and bending under the weight of something he carried on his back. He was surprised to see any human being in this lonely and unfrequented place, but supposing it to be some one of the neighborhood in need of his assistance, he hastened down to yield it.*
>
> *On nearer approach he was still more surprised at the singularity of the stranger's appearance. He was a short square-built old fellow, with thick bushy hair, and a grizzled beard. His dress was of the antique Dutch fashion— a cloth jerkin strapped round the waist—several pair of*

breeches, the outer one of ample volume, decorated with rows of buttons down the sides, and bunches at the knees. He bore on his shoulder a stout keg, that seemed full of liquor, and made signs for Rip to approach and assist him with the load.

1. Is any of the dialogue in the short story used as dialogue in the play? What thought in the short story is expressed in the play by sound effects and a monologue, or speech that Rip makes to himself?

2. How does the playwright present the information in the second paragraph of the above excerpt? Identify at least two elements of plays that she uses.

Now check your answers with your teacher. Review this part of the lesson if you don't understand why an answer was incorrect.

 WRITING ON YOUR OWN 1

In this exercise you will begin to develop the elements of a folktale that will work in play form. Follow these steps:

* For each of the tales you listed in the first writing exercise, decide which characters are essential for the plot. List the characters on the sheet for that tale.
* Consider the settings in each fairy tale or folktale. Which of the settings would be attractive on a stage? What scenery would be needed? What props? Make a list on each sheet, describing the settings you would use.
* Consider the plot of each tale. Which events involve exciting action or funny scenes or memorable dialogue? Which scenes would you like to put on stage much as they are in the original story? List these scenes on each sheet.
* Save your sheets for the next writing exercise.

LESSON 2 | REPLACING WHAT DOESN'T WORK ON STAGE

As you probably noted when comparing the play with the short story excerpts in Lesson 1, Adele Thane does not use all of Washington Irving's details. Irving relates that Rip had illustrious ancestors, but there is no mention of this in the play. The information doesn't have any effect on the plot, so Thane leaves it out. Irving also points out that Rip was "a great favorite among all the good wives of the village"—other than his own wife, of course. But the play version does not include any other wives. Again, Thane omits a detail that has no bearing on what happens to Rip.

Besides leaving out details that are unnecessary to the plot, Thane also changes some more important matters. Why? Read this excerpt from Irving's short story and see if you can figure out some reasons. When you have finished, review pages 236 to 238 of the play. Determine Thane's major changes in the scene. Why do you suppose she felt these changes were necessary?

> *What seemed particularly odd to Rip was, that though these folks were evidently amusing themselves, yet they maintained the gravest faces, the most mysterious silence, and were, withal, the most melancholy party of pleasure he had ever witnessed. Nothing interrupted the stillness of the scene but the noise of the balls, which, whenever they were rolled, echoed along the mountains like rumbling peals of thunder.*
>
> *As Rip and his companion approached them, they suddenly desisted from their play, and stared at him with such fixed statue-like gaze . . . that his heart turned within him, and his knees smote together. His companion now emptied the contents of the keg into large flagons, and made signs to him to wait upon the company. He obeyed with fear and trembling; they quaffed [drank] the liquor in profound silence, and then returned to their game.*
>
> *By degrees Rip's awe and apprehension subsided.*

He even ventured, when no eye was fixed upon him, to taste the beverage, which he found had much of the flavor of excellent Hollands. He was naturally a thirsty soul, and was soon tempted to repeat the draught [take another drink]. One taste provoked another; and he reiterated [repeated] his visits to the flagon so often that at length his senses were overpowered, his eyes swam in his head, his head gradually declined, and he fell into a deep sleep.

Irving's strangers are silent, and after their first mute inspection of Rip, they ignore him. How would that play on the stage? Audience members might be confused by what was happening. They might even suspect that the actors had forgotten their lines. They probably would be bored or confused by the silence. Even though this scene is a major part of the plot, it would have little impact on a stage. So to give the scene the attention it requires, Thane gives Hudson's crew voices, personalities, and a much more obvious interest in Rip.

Another difference between the short story and the play is that some of the action of the short story occurs at Rip's home. However, that action is not important and can be mentioned in dialogue or omitted altogether. The playwright decided that having another set, with scenery that showed a little house and unkempt yard, would distract from the major scenes.

It is up to the playwright to interpret the main ideas of a short story for the stage. Wherever techniques or details in the short story interfere with the effectiveness of the play, they must be adjusted or replaced.

EXERCISE 2

Read the following passage from the short story and compare it with the end of the play (pages 241-242). Then use what you have learned in this lesson to answer the questions that follow.

"What is your name, my good woman?" asked he.

"Judith Gardenier."

"And your father's name?"

"Ah, poor man, Rip Van Winkle was his name, but it's twenty years since he went away from home with his gun, and never has been heard of since—his dog came home without him; but whether he shot himself, or was carried away by the Indians, nobody can tell. I was then but a little girl."

Rip had but one question more to ask; but he put it with a faltering voice:

"Where's your mother?"

"Oh, she too had died but a short time since; she broke a blood-vessel in a fit of passion at a New-England peddler."

There was a drop of comfort, at least, in this intelligence. The honest man could contain himself no longer. He caught his daughter and her child in his arms. "I am your father!" cried he. "Young Rip Van Winkle once—old Rip Van Winkle now!—Does nobody know poor Rip Van Winkle?"

All stood amazed, until an old woman, tottering out from among the crowd, put her hand to her brow, and peering under it in his face for a moment, exclaimed, "Sure enough! it is Rip Van Winkle—it is himself! Welcome home again, old neighbor—Why, where have you been these twenty long years?"

1. Who first recognizes Rip in the short story? Who first recognizes him in the play? How does each of these people identify Rip? Which method is more dramatic, making better use of stage techniques? Explain your answer.

2. The short story reports Rip's reaction to the news of his wife's death this way: "There was a drop of comfort, at least, in this intelligence." Compare this sentence with Rip's reaction in the play. Why did the playwright change Rip's reaction?

Now check your answers with your teacher. Review this part of the lesson if you don't understand why an answer was incorrect.

WRITING ON YOUR OWN 2

In this exercise you will use what you have learned to determine what elements of a fairy tale or folktale you would need to change to make a good play. Follow these steps:

• Review your notes from Developing an Adaptation and Writing on Your Own 1. Of the three or more tales you have been considering, choose one to continue developing.
• Review the plot of your chosen tale. If you have a written version of the tale, reread it. If you are working from memory, recall the order of the events of the plot as best you can. Are there some events that require a good deal of background information or explanations of what the characters are thinking? How can you present the necessary information in a dramatic form? Maybe you'll need to invent a new scene or a new character who can tell your hero some news. Perhaps your hero needs a companion with whom to share his or her thoughts. On your notepaper, or an additional sheet, describe changes that you think would make your adaptation more affective.

LESSON 3 LOOKING AT THE RESULTS

When a popular book or short story is adapted for the stage, people who are very familiar with the original version often compare the two works. They may be tempted to say, "The play is different from the book. Therefore it is not a good adaptation." However, as you have seen, fiction and plays have different needs and requirements. A good stage adaptation cannot stick to the original work of fiction in every way. So how much must be picked up? How much change is allowed? There are no easy answers and strict rules. There are a few commonsense guidelines, however.

First, adaptations always should stay true to what made the original work popular. For example, if the original ends with the tragic deaths of the hero and heroine, the adaptation must not have a happy ending. If an important theme of the original is that greed hurts the cheaters as much as it hurts their victims, the adaptation must not justify greed. If the original was noted for its lively sense of humor, the adaptation should have lively humor, too, even if its jokes are different.

Second, the adaptation must make effective use of the special characteristics of plays. For example, its scenery, props, and costumes should suggest a place and time effectively. Its lighting and sound effects should contribute to the mood. Its dialogue should reveal characters and conflicts accurately. Its stage directions should emphasize important actions and attitudes.

To judge Thane's *Rip Van Winkle*, then, you can apply these two guidelines to it. Does it communicate a sense of what gives the Irving story lasting popularity? Does it make effective use of the special characteristics of plays?

Review the scene from the play in which Rip tells the children about Hendrik Hudson and his crew (page 233). Then read this excerpt from the original story, which follows Rip's return to town. What tone and theme do the two passages share?

> *Peter was the most ancient inhabitant of the village, and well versed in all the wonderful events and traditions of the neighborhood. He recollected Rip at once, and corroborated [backed up] his story in the most satisfactory manner. He assured the company that it was a fact, handed down from his ancestor the historian, that the Kaatskill Mountains had always been haunted by strange beings. That it was affirmed [recognized] that the great*

Hendrick Hudson, the first discoverer of the river and country, kept a kind of vigil there every twenty years, with his crew of the Half-Moon; being permitted in this way to revisit the scenes of his enterprise, and keep a guardian eye upon the river, and the great city called by his name. That his father had once seen them in their old Dutch dresses playing at nine-pins in a hollow of the mountain; and that he himself had heard, one summer afternoon, the sound of their balls, like distant peals of thunder.

The story of Hendrik Hudson appears at different points in the two plots, and it is told by different characters. However, the adaptation brings out the same effect as the original: they both call on our sense of wonder about nature and our delight at magical explanations. The play gives a voice to many in the audience when little Jacob declares, "I wish I could see Hendrik Hudson and his crew."

EXERCISE 3

Review the last scene of the play, after Judith recognizes her father (page 242). Then read this excerpt that ends the short story. Use what you have learned to answer the questions that follow.

He used to tell his story to every stranger that arrived at Mr. Doolittle's hotel. He was observed, at first, to vary on some points every time he told it, which was, doubtless, owing to his having so recently awaked. It at last settled down precisely to the tale I have related, and not a man, woman, or child in the neighborhood, but knew it by heart. Some always pretended to doubt the reality of it, and insisted that Rip had been out of his head, and that this was one point on which he always remained flighty. The old Dutch inhabitants, however, almost universally gave it full credit. Even to this day they never hear a thunderstorm of a summer afternoon about the

Kaatskill, but they say Hendrick Hudson and his crew are at their game of nine-pins; and it is a common wish of all hen-pecked husbands in the neighborhood, when life hangs heavy on their hands, that they might have a quieting draught [drink] out of Rip Van Winkle's flagon.

1. How seriously does either version take itself? Is either version trying to teach a lesson? If not, what purpose do you infer from each ending?

2. Look again at the very ending of the play. What techniques does the playwright use to give the play a strong finish?

Now check your answers with your teacher. Review this part of the lesson if you don't understand why an answer was incorrect.

WRITING ON YOUR OWN 3

So far, you have considered the elements of a folktale or fairy tale that would work well on stage. Now you will focus on the original tale. Follow these steps:

- In Writing on Your Own 2, you chose a folktale or fairy tale to adapt into a play. Think back to the reasons for your decision. What did you like about your chosen tale? Was it the plot? characters? mood? theme? something else?
- Review your notes for the tale you are adapting. Have you discussed the element that makes the tale special for you? If so, put a star or a check next to that section of your notes. That will remind you to take special care with that element when you write your adaptation. You'll want to make it important to your audience, just as it is to you. If you haven't made any notes about that element yet, consider how you can bring it out in the dialogue or stage directions of your play. Add your ideas to your planning sheet.
- Save your planning sheet for your final writing exercise.

DISCUSSION GUIDES

1. Rip tells the children that thunder is the sound of bowling balls being rolled by Hendrik Hudson's crew. Have you heard any other made-up stories that explain happenings in nature, or how certain mountains, rivers, or other places came to be? Tell the story as you remember it to your class or to a small group of classmates. Has anyone else heard an explanation similar to yours?

2. Rip's friends at the tavern blamed Dame Van Winkle for making life unpleasant for Rip. How much of her bad temper was caused by Rip himself? What would you have told Rip to do to improve the situation? What would you have advised Dame Van Winkle to do to improve the situation? Can your class agree on two or three suggestions for each partner in that marriage?

3. Imagine that Rip woke up this morning from his twenty-year sleep. What important events would he have missed during the last two decades? If he wandered into your classroom, on what topics would you bring him up-to-date? With a small group, make a list of the top ten happenings of the last twenty years in your city and state, in your country, and in the world. Afterward, compare lists with other groups. Be ready to explain and defend your choices.

ADAPT A FOLKTALE OR FAIRY TALE TO THE STAGE

In this unit you have analyzed how well several folktales or fairy tales can be adapted for dramatic presentation. Now you will use what you have learned in the lessons to adapt one of those tales for the stage.

If you have questions about the writing process, refer to Using the Writing Process (page 261).

- Assemble the writing you did for this unit, including 1) notes about the purpose, audience, and possible promotional approach for several plays based on folktales or fairy tales; 2) notes on characters, settings, and plot developments that you would use in a play version; 3) notes on changes you would make to the original tale to make it more effective on stage; 4) notes on the characteristics that make the original tale special, and which you want to keep.
- Think about the folktale or fairy tale you have chosen to adapt. Review your notes on what can be used, what must be changed, and what is special about the original tale.
- Make an outline of the scenes you will use. For each scene, note the setting, the characters involved, and a few sentences about the action. Remember to limit your settings and to make sure you have included all the necessary events in the plot.
- Write your play, using the format shown throughout the plays in this book. Remember to describe the setting at the beginning of each scene. Be sure to use stage directions wherever they are needed, and to put them in parentheses and underline them to set them off.
- Ask one or more classmates to read through the play with you, taking the characters' parts and walking through the motions described in the stage directions. Use what you learn during the reading and from your classmates' comments to revise your play as needed.
- Proofread your play for spelling, grammar, punctuation, capitalization, and formatting errors, and then make a final copy. If possible, have your same classmates help perform your final play for the rest of the class.

USING THE WRITING PROCESS

This reference section explains the major steps in the writing process. It will help you complete the writing exercises in this book. Read the information carefully so you can understand the process thoroughly. Whenever you need a quick review of important things to think about when you write, refer to the handy checklist on page 267.

Most tasks worth doing have several steps. For example, houses can be built only after the builder follows a number of complicated, logical steps. Moviemakers must go through a series of steps before releasing a film. Even a task as simple as making a peanut butter and jelly sandwich requires that the sandwich maker perform specific steps in order. So it should be no surprise that anyone who wants to write a good story, play, poem, report, or article must follow certain steps too. Taken together, the steps a writer follows are called the *writing process*. This writing process is divided into three main stages: prewriting, writing, and revising. Each stage is important for good writing.

STAGE 1: Prewriting

Prewriting consists of all the preparation you do before you put a single word down on paper. There are many decisions that you must make in order to make your writing as interesting, logical, and easy to read as possible. Here are the steps you should take before you begin to write:

1. **Decide on your audience.** Who will read your writing? Will your audience be your teacher? Will it be readers of the school newspaper? Or will your audience be family or friends? Your writing will change, depending on who you think your audience will be.

2. **Decide on your purpose.** Why are you writing? Do you want to teach your audience something? Do you want to entertain

them? Do you want to change someone's mind about an issue? Think about your purpose before you begin to write.

3. **Think about possible topics.** What are some topics that interest you? Make a list of topics that you are familiar with and might like to write about. Make another list of topics that interest you and that you want to learn about.

    One technique that helps some writers at this stage is *brainstorming.* When you brainstorm, you let your mind wander freely. Without judging your ideas first, scribble them down as they come to you—even if they seem silly or farfetched. Good ideas often develop from unusual thoughts.

    If you're having trouble coming up with ideas by yourself, brainstorm with a partner or a group of classmates. Jot down everyone's ideas as they say them. Brainstorming alone or with others should give you a long list of possible writing topics.

4. **Choose and narrow your topic.** Once you have chosen a topic, you will probably find that it is impossible to cover every aspect of it in one piece of writing. Say, for example, you have chosen to write about the possibility of life on other planets. In a single piece of writing   you could not possibly include everything that has been researched about extraterrestrial life. Therefore you must choose one or two aspects to focus on, such as alleged sightings in the United States or worldwide organizations that study extraterrestrial life. Otherwise you might overload your writing with too many ideas. Concentrate on telling about a few things thoroughly and well.

5. **Research your topic.** You probably have had experience using an encyclopedia, the library, or the Internet to look up information for factual reports. But even when you write fictional stories, you often need to do some research. In a story set during the Civil War, for example, your characters

wouldn't use pocket cameras or wear suits of armor. In order to make your story as accurate and believable as possible, you would have to research how Americans lived and dressed during the years of the Civil War.

To conduct your research, you may want to use books, magazines, newspapers, reference works, or electronic sources. Some topics may require you to interview knowledgeable people. For realistic stories set in the present time, you may find that the best research is simple observation of everyday life. Thorough research will help ensure that your facts and details are accurate.

6. **Organize your research.** Once you have the facts, ideas, and details you need to decide how to arrange them. Which order will you choose? No matter what you are writing, it is always helpful to begin with a written plan. If you are writing a story, you probably will tell it in time order. Make a list of the major story events, arranged from first to last.

Arranging details in time order is not the only way to organize information, however. Some writers start by making *lists* (informal outlines) of the facts and ideas they have gathered. Then they rearrange the items on their lists until they have the order that will work well in their writing.

Other writers make formal *outlines,* designating the most important ideas with roman numerals (I, II, III, IV, and so on) and related details with letters and numerals (A, B, C; 1, 2, 3; a, b, c; and so on). An outline is a more formal version of a list, and like the items in a list, the items in an outline can be rearranged until you decide on a logical order. Both outlines and lists help you organize and group your ideas.

Mapping or *clustering* is another helpful technique used by many writers. With this method, you write a main idea in the center of a cluster and then surround it with facts and ideas connected to that idea. Following is an example of a cluster map:

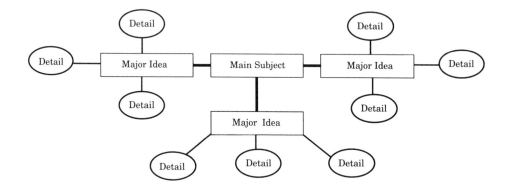

STAGE 2: **Writing**

1. **Get started.** Begin your writing with an introductory sentence or paragraph. A good introduction can become a guide for the rest of your piece. For ideas on good opening sentences, take a look at some of your favorite stories or magazine articles.

   Your introduction should give your audience a hint about what is coming next. If you are writing a story, your introduction should set the tone and mood. It should reveal the narrator's point of view, and it may introduce the main characters, the setting, and your purpose for writing. Do the best you can with your introduction, but remember that, if you wish to, you can always change it later.

2. **Keep writing.** Get your thoughts down as quickly as possible, referring to your prewriting notes to keep you on track. Later, when you are done with this *rough draft,* you will have a chance to revise and polish your work to make it as clear and accurate as possible. For right now, however, don't stop for spelling, grammar, or exact wording problems. Come as close as you can to what you want to say but don't let yourself get bogged down in details.

STAGE 3: Revising

Now you're ready to revise your work. Careful revision includes editing and reorganizing that can make a big difference in the final product. You may wish to get feedback from your classmates or your teacher about how to revise your work.

1. **Revise and edit your work.** When you are revising and editing, ask yourself these questions:
   - Did I follow my prewriting plan? Reread your entire first draft. Compare it to your original plan. Did you skip anything important? If you added an idea, did it work logically with the rest of your plan? Even if you decide that your prewriting plan is no longer what you want, it may include ideas you don't want to lose.
   - Is my writing clear and logical? Does one idea follow the other in a sensible order? Do you want to change the order or add ideas to make the organization clearer?
   - Is my language clear and interesting? Have you chosen exact verbs, nouns, and adjectives? For example, have you used forms of the verb to be (is, are, being, become) more often than you should? If so, replace them or change your sentence to make them unnecessary. Include precise action words such as raced, hiked, zoomed, and hurried in place of the overused verb went. Instead of using vague nouns such as water and green, choose exact ones such as cascade or pond and lime. Replace common adjectives such as beautiful and nice with precise ones such as elegant, gorgeous, and lovely.
   - Is my writing clear and to the point? Take out words that repeat the same ideas. For example, don't use both liberty and freedom. These words are synonyms. Choose one word or the other.

2. **Proofread for errors in spelling, grammar, capitalization, and punctuation.** Anyone reading your writing will notice such

errors immediately. These errors can confuse your readers or make them lose interest in what they are reading.

If you are in doubt about the spelling of a word, look it up or ask someone for help. If you are unsure about your grammar, read your writing aloud and listen carefully. Does anything sound wrong? Check with a friend or class-mate if you need a second opinion—or refer to a grammar handbook.

Make sure every group of words is a complete sentence. Are any of your sentences run-ons? Do proper nouns begin with capital letters? Is the first word of every sentence capitalized? Do all your sentences have the correct end marks? Should you add any other punctuation to your writing to make your ideas even clearer? If your writing includes dialogue, have you used quotation marks correctly?

3. **Make a clean final draft to share.** After you are satisfied with your writing, it is time to share it with your audience. If you are lucky enough to be composing on a computer, you can print out a final copy easily, after running a spell-check. If you are writing your final draft by hand, make sure your handwriting is clear and easy to read. Leave margins on either side of the page. You may want to skip every other line. Make your writing look inviting to your readers. After all, you put a lot of work into this piece. It's important that someone read and enjoy it.

A WRITING CHECKLIST

Ask yourself these questions before beginning a writing assignment:

- Have I chosen a topic that is both interesting and manageable? Should I narrow it so I can cover it in the space that I have?
- Do I have a clear prewriting plan?
- What should I do to gather my facts and ideas? read? interview? observe?
- How will I organize my ideas? a list? an outline? a cluster map?
- Do I have an opening sentence or paragraph that will pull my readers in?
- Do I need to add more information? Switch the order of paragraphs? Take out unnecessary information?

Ask yourself these questions after completing a writing assignment:

- Did I use my prewriting plan?
- Is the organization of my writing clear? Should I move, add, or delete any paragraphs or sentences to make the ideas flow more logically?
- Do all the sentences in one paragraph relate to one idea?
- Have I used active, precise words? Is my language interesting? Do the words say what I mean to say?
- Are all the words spelled correctly?
- Have I used correct grammar, capitalization, punctuation, and formatting?
- Is my final draft legible, clean, and attractive?

GLOSSARY OF LITERARY TERMS

This glossary includes definitions for important literary terms that are introduced in this book. Boldfaced words within the definitions are other terms that appear in the glossary.

act   a major section of a play. An act can be further divided into several smaller sections called **scenes**.

adaptation   the process by which a literary work is changed from one form into another form—for example, from a short story to a play.

cast of characters   all the **characters** who appear in a play. A play's characters are usually listed in the order in which they appear on stage.

characterization   the methods by which a writer develops a particular character's personality. Four common methods of characterization are (1) giving a physical description of a character, (2) telling what the character says and does, (3) revealing the character's thoughts, and (4) revealing how others feel about the character.

characters   the people who act and speak in a play. The word *character* also refers to the personality of each individual. Characters in a play are portrayed by actors.

climax   the point of highest tension or greatest interest in a story or play. The climax is usually the turning point in the **plot.** From that point, the probable outcome of the story or play becomes clear.

conflict   a struggle or tension between opposing forces that is central to a **plot.**

dialogue   all the words spoken by the actors in a play. Dialogue helps move the **plot** along and also reveals the personalities of the **characters.**

downstage   the area of a stage that is nearest the audience.

drama a kind of literature designed for the theater and meant to be performed in front of an audience. Actors take the roles of the **characters,** perform the assigned actions, and speak the written words.

exposition the part of a **plot** in which the playwright introduces the **characters** and **conflicts** and provides whatever background information is necessary. The exposition often presents information about the **setting** also.

falling action the part of a **plot** in which the tension eases and the action begins to slow down. The falling action leads to a **resolution.**

introduction *See* **exposition.**

mood the general feeling or atmosphere of a play.

narration the writing that gives the events and actions of the story.

narrator the person who is telling a story. The narrator speaks directly to the audience.

pace the overall rate of speed at which the speeches and actions of a play are performed.

play a literary work that tells a story through the characters' words and actions. A play is meant to be performed in front of an audience.

plot the sequence of events in a piece of writing. A plot usually has five sections: **exposition** or introduction, **rising action, climax, falling action,** and **resolution.**

props the movable articles used in a play, other than costumes and **scenery.** The word *props* is a shortened version of *properties*.

resolution the last part of a **plot;** the conclusion of a play. The resolution contains the outcome of the **conflict.**

rising action the part of a **plot** in which tension builds and complications develop. During the rising action, the **conflict** increases and the action moves toward the **climax.**

scene　a section of a play that occurs in one place and at one time. A new scene begins each time there is a change in either. Frequently, several scenes make up a single **act.**

scenery　the backdrop on a stage that identifies a play's **setting,** or time and place.

set　a combination of **scenery** and **props** that establish the **setting** and the **mood.**

setting　the time and place of the action of a story or play. Many playwrights establish the setting of a play through **stage directions** in the **exposition.**

sound effects　the sounds called for in the script of a play, radio or television program, or motion picture.

stage directions　any information that is intended for the director, the actors, or the readers of a play. Stage directions are separate from the **dialogue** and are often printed in *italics*.

stage left　the part of a stage that is on the left from the actors' point of view. The audience sees it as the right side of the stage.

stage right　the part of a stage that is on the right from the actors' point of view. The audience sees it as the left side of the stage.

staging　everything that an audience sees and hears during a play. Staging covers decisions about costumes, **scenery, props,** actors' movements on stage, and **sound effects.**

storyboard　a series of pictures depicting the important events in a plot. Storyboards are often used by movie directors for reference throughout the filming of a screenplay.

style   the distinctive way in which something is written, said, or acted.

theme   the underlying message or central idea of a piece of writing.

tone   a writer's attitude toward the subject or the audience.

upstage   the area of a stage that is farthest from the audience.